RTI
ROADMAP
FOR SCHOOL LEADERS

TRANSFORMATIONAL
LEARNING

RTI
ROADMAP
FOR SCHOOL LEADERS

PLAN AND GO ►

TOM HIERCK
CHRIS WEBER

LEAD+
LEARN
PRESS

ENGLEWOOD, COLORADO

The Leadership and Learning Center
5680 Greenwood Plaza Boulevard, Suite 550
Greenwood Village, Colorado 80111
Phone 1.866.399.6019 | Fax 303.504.9417
www.leadandlearn.com

Published by Lead + Learn Press.

Cataloging-in-Publication Data

Hierck, Tom, 1960-
  RTI roadmap for school leaders : plan and go / Tom Hierck, Chris Weber.
  pages cm
  Includes bibliographical references and index.
  ISBN 978-1-935588-47-4
    1. Response to intervention (Learning disabled children)   I. Weber, Chris
(Chris A.)   II. Title.   III. Title: RTI roadmap for school leaders.
  LC4705.H54 2014   371.9'043
                                                                          QBI14-600085

ISBN 978-1-935588-47-4

Printed in the United States of America

   02 03 04 05 06   19 18 17 16 15 14

4500517388   A B C D E F G

To the many students I've had the good fortune
to work with over the past thirty years,
and the dedicated educators
who inspired and enlightened me.

TOM HIERCK

To my sister, Kelly,
my best friend and inspiration.

CHRIS WEBER

Contents

Acknowledgments

Although only two names appear on the front cover of this book, many heads and hands guided our work. We are indebted to colleagues who allowed us the opportunity to work through the content of this book as we were engaged in the revision process. Finding success in schools with educators and students strengthened the work that you are about to read through. In particular we'd like to thank Christine Day and Anthony Little (Hale County, Alabama), Becky Brothers-McGowan and Donna Martin (Blount County, Alabama), and Greg Wolcott (Woodridge, Illinois).

We also owe a debt of gratitude to Alan Bernhard and Carrie Williams at Boulder Bookworks for their insights as we developed the manuscript. Finally, a number of wonderful colleagues at The Leadership and Learning Center / Houghton Mifflin Harcourt provided feedback and support along the way. Thanks to Lisa Almeida, Jess Engman, Tony Flach, Lissa Pijanowski, and Angela Peery for your shared wisdom.

Introduction

Response to Intervention (RTI) is best understood as the practices (such as those related to instructional delivery, assessment, and student discipline) and processes (related to the daily, weekly, or monthly routines of educators, such as schedules, collaborative times, and methods of communicating) that impact and are impacted by virtually everything we do in education. RTI is about using the knowledge, skills, and attributes of all members of a learning organization to positively impact the life chances of all students. We have too often lowered our expectations, in most cases subconsciously, on the basis of socioeconomic status, ethnicity, number of parents, or some other external variable. RTI has the power to address and reverse these historical injustices. We believe that schools can and absolutely will make a difference in the lives of *all* students. RTI is not about waiting until all other options are exhausted and then hoping to deploy some sort of rescue mission. It is not about providing a last chance on the road to academic failure. RTI represents proactive efforts to ensure that students receive the supports they need as soon as they show signs of struggle with academic or behavioral expectations. It is built on the premise that all students can learn and achieve at high levels and that educators will provide the necessary supports and time needed to ensure that this happens.

A quick survey of education literature reveals a significant number of books and guides related to Response to Intervention (or Instruction). A Google search for "Response to Intervention" generates millions of results. While it is not likely that all of these will generate high-quality information, the sheer volume does indicate how quickly the education scene has embraced the notion of RTI. We believe that school administrators and faculty *want* to do RTI and know they *need* to do RTI. This belief is based on our more than fifty years of combined experience as educators at all grade levels working with students across the academic and behavioral spectrum. Between us, we have worked with United States educators in the vast majority of the 50 states and also with educators in every province and territory in Canada. Gaining insight into what works, what needs to be adjusted, and what needs to be abandoned has allowed us to collaborate in hundreds of schools with thousands of educators to create localized, contextualized responses that stand the best chance of being both sustainable and successful. Our work in the field has highlighted for us that, frequently, school teams don't know what they need to do and don't know where to start. School leaders want and need someone to craft a model *with* them; they don't want someone to preach at them or simply tell them what to do. Our experiences are the motivation behind the RTI Roadmap approach—a customized strategic solution that embraces collaborative and ongoing professional development as an indispensable asset. The intent is to craft a solution that is uniquely contextualized to the school and that matches the mission and vision of that school. The emphasis is on "transformational learning" (learning that generates long-term change and benefit, and which may affect the learner's future experiences) as opposed to "transactional learning" (learning that is in the moment or for a specific purpose and doesn't necessarily connect to future learning).

Take a moment to think about a student that challenges you the most (behaviorally, academically, or a little of both) and what the future holds for that student if we, as educators and school leaders, don't intervene. The information in Figure I.1 from Statistic Brain (2014) provides a bleak outlook about the likely outcomes for dropouts.

The impacts associated with dropping out of school are dire indeed. These tragic realities highlight the moral imperative to ensure that all students achieve at least a high school diploma. It is likely that in this era students will need to carry their ability to learn beyond high school to ensure a viable future. Despite this knowledge, and the fact that the preponderance of data suggests we need to improve our

FIGURE I.1 United States High School Dropout Statistics	
Total number of high school dropouts annually	3,030,000
Number of high school students who drop out each day	8,300
Percent of Americans with a high school diploma	85.3%
Percent of all dropouts that happen in the ninth grade	36%
Percent of students who repeat ninth grade that go on to graduate	15%
Percent of students in 50 largest U.S. cities that graduate from high school	59%
Percent of U.S. crimes committed by a high school dropout	75%
Difference in lifetime income between high school graduate and dropout	$260,000
Percent of U.S. jobs for which a high school dropout is not eligible	90%

success rates, the struggle to implement RTI continues in many jurisdictions. Buffum, Mattos, and Weber (2012) express this frustration accurately: "Yet in spite of this knowledge, most schools continue to struggle to meet the needs of all their students, especially the ones most at risk. Most schools continue to function like one-room schoolhouses, with individual teachers responsible only for "their" kids" (p. 2).

It's clear we know what will happen to students if we don't intervene. Moreover, it's not a question of knowing what to do. Ron Edmonds (1979) understood this many years ago: "We can, whenever and wherever we choose, successfully teach all children whose schooling is of interest to us," he said (p. 23). The knowledge and potential exists in every school in which we've worked. We can and must develop the attributes, attitudes, and abilities that all students will need to make a successful transition to college or a skilled career. Our work as educators is to ensure that this outcome is met.

RTI OVERVIEW

Before launching into the specific components of the RTI Roadmap, it may be instructive to offer a quick review of RTI. The reauthorization and amendment of the Individuals with Disabilities Education Improvement Act (IDEA) in 2004 altered the landscape for schools. Whereas practitioners previously used the IQ-achievement discrepancy model to identify children with learning disabilities, the reauthorization allowed schools to employ a lack of "Response to Intervention," or RTI, as an alternative method for determining eligibility for special education and as a rationale for providing early intervention to children at risk for school failure. While the reauthorized law seems, at first glance, to relate to eligibility determinations for special education, using a lack of response to intervention for such determinations has obvious implications for all of education. RTI implies that we must *intervene* and monitor the extent to which students are *responding*. IDEA 2004 encourages this intervention and monitoring to be done early—early in a student's school career (in grades K–3) and also early upon the identification of a difficulty or deficit—and permits districts to use as much as 15 percent of their special education monies to fund these early intervention services.

Response to Intervention is a framework for achieving the ongoing improvement of student outcomes (Buffum, Mattos, and Weber, 2009, 2010, and 2012; Hierck, Coleman, and Weber, 2011). It is a school-wide construct that provides high-quality instruction and research-based systematic interventions for all student needs—academic, social-emotional, and behavioral. From struggling students striving to meet minimum proficiency to gifted students striving to reach their potential, RTI invites a partnership among students, teachers, parents, and the community whereby all students achieving positive outcomes is the priority.

Unfortunately, challenges remain, and they are largely due to a lack of clarity about the positive impact of a well-constructed approach to RTI that can be realized by all schools. Some schools have gone to the extreme interpretation of IDEA and have used RTI simply as an identification/qualification tool as they fast-track students out of regular instruction and into special education. In effect, they use the skills of their specialized teachers to impose a sentence on students rather than an intervention. Using RTI to meet compliance audits, to raise a school's test scores by taking struggling students out of the mainstream, or to rationalize a view that "our students are less able/more challenging" completely undermines the value of the work and reduces it to just another "flavor of the month," allowing cynicism to rise and the hard work of positive, productive change to remain shelved until the crisis of underperformance becomes too large to ignore. Buffum, Mattos, and Weber (2012) frame it thusly: "While the specific obstacles vary, the underlying cause of the problem is the same: too many schools have failed to develop the correct *thinking* about Response to Intervention."

The critical components of an effective RTI system are:

► High-quality instruction and learning opportunities for all students.

► Identification of students struggling to meet grade-level expectations.

► Attention to the learning rates and levels of performance for all students.

► Increasing intensity and targetedness of instruction/ intervention based on identified student needs.

► Data-informed decision making using the skills of the team to solve problems.

The process of RTI involves screening for at-risk students, monitoring the responsiveness of students to instruction and intervention, and problem solving to determine the appropriate course of action.

The latter two steps are repeated as necessary until educators see the desired outcomes achieved. Within an RTI-based system of supports, students who are struggling are identified in a proactive and timely manner and teams determine early intervention solutions to minimize the impact of struggles. This information is garnered by assessing student response to high-quality instruction that has been demonstrated to be effective. In this sense, RTI emphasizes "student outcomes instead of student deficits" (Kavale, Holdnack, and Mostert, 2005, p. 4). RTI is equally impactful for students who are not identified as struggling, but who are considered gifted or above level, but whose needs may not be met. RTI must be applied to *all* students; educators must work to ensure that every student has access to appropriate learning experiences.

Targeted intervention *supplements*—it does not *replace*—the general education, or Tier 1, program of instruction. Student response to the intervention is used to determine a further course of action. If students respond to the intervention, supports are continued until gaps are eliminated. If students do not respond in a timely manner, they are provided with a different, more intense set of supports. Their progress is again monitored and further actions determined. Here is a quick review of the three tiers of intervention:

TIER 1

► Engaging, differentiated instruction for *all* students

► Multiple opportunities to respond to instruction

► Immediate corrective feedback

► Scaffolded practice of new skills

► Cumulative review of previously taught skills

► Daily 10- to 15-minute small-group supports to more homogenous groups of students based on need

TIER 2

► More time and differentiated supports for students who have not mastered the essentials, as measured by regular common formative assessments

► May be provided during daily 30-minute flex times or during "buffer" days

► Students grouped more homogeneously during these flex times

► Students who have not yet mastered essentials receive support in smaller groups, from the teacher who has had the most success, as measured by the common formative assessments

► Other staff may join the grade-level teachers to reduce teacher-student ratio during flex time

► To make optimal use of additional staff, schools may choose to stagger times during which each grade level has flex time

► Purpose of Tier 2 is for students to master prioritized grade-level or course content

TIER 3

► For students who have not responded to Tier 1 and Tier 2 supports

► For students who have been screened to be multiple grade levels behind their peers in foundational skills

► Intensive supports provided in addition to Tier 1 and 2 supports

► Supports are as targeted as possible; e.g., on phonemic awareness, single-syllable phonics, or multisyllabic phonics

► Given the constraints of the school's schedule and the immediacy and severity of student needs, Tier 3 supports may need to be provided, temporarily, in place of other important content

▬ Schools can creatively schedule these supports:

– Providing them when students would otherwise be working independently, such as during workshop, center, or "daily five" time

– Alternating what content that the student misses from week to week

– Providing these supports when students are not receiving instruction in the essentials of the grade level

► The support should be adjusted to match student needs and revised until the student is adequately responding to intervention.

Just as educators must assess the effectiveness of their Tier 1 instructional programs, they must also continually evaluate the success of their interventions. Tiers vary in intensity, instructor expertise, and size of student groupings, but all must employ research-validated instructional strategies. Fuchs and Fuchs (2006) outline two intervention approaches: the problem-solving method and the standard treatment (or protocol) method. Educators generally use the problem-solving method, while those doing research most often employ the standard treatment method. The problem-solving approach allows for interventions to occur within the classroom and is individualized to the student. This approach is based on the belief that the success of an intervention cannot be predicted based on generalized student characteristics, and that there is not a "one size fits all" solution. The process involves problem identification, selection of an appropriate intervention, implementation of that intervention, and monitoring of response. Problem-solving teams include a range of personnel, including general educators, special educators, administrators, and school psychologists. The standard treatment or protocol method, unlike the problem-solving approach, typically prescribes pre-determined interventions based on established criteria. While we under-stand the rationale behind the standard treatment method and appreciate the norms that it provides, we favor a problem-solving ap-proach and will describe that approach in this book.

RTI is appropriate for all students and all educators who support and inform effective practices. Success is based on the authentic and committed collaboration of all adults who are connected to students. Ultimately, RTI is something you do and not something you buy. While not speaking specifically about RTI, noted educator Benjamin Bloom captured the essence of this work: "... modern society requires continual learning throughout life. If the schools do not promote ad-equate learning and reassurance of progress, the student must come to reject learning—both in school and later life" (p. 11). That this was uttered in 1968 should serve as both a reminder and an immediate call to action.

As with any guidebook, some factors need to be taken into con-sideration when beginning a journey using the RTI Roadmap:

► What's our destination?

► What's our starting point?

► Who's "driving" (the change or desired outcome)?

► Who's with us on the trip?

This roadmap will provide guidance while enabling educators to make midcourse adjustments and bring context to the journey. Failure to anticipate the need for adjustments reduces the effectiveness of RTI and devalues it to just another checklist of things to do. The promise of RTI will not be realized with passively compliant behavior, but in-stead through deliberate action by committed educators that will alter outcomes for students. The successful implementation of RTI requires two things from a school or district and the educators who populate it—a redefined set of tools to help students learn and a new way of thinking about their responsibility to ensure this outcome is met.

What makes a good roadmap? Good roadmaps present under-standable steps that lead travelers to critical decision points. A roadmap sets clear future objectives and answers the critical why, what, and how questions to create a plan for reaching that objective. The "why" questions define objectives and strategies, the "what" questions are about challenges, solutions, and performance targets, and the "how" questions outline the processes and resources (human and technical) that will be needed along the way. With these questions answered, teams can develop their action plans. This book is structured around key sections of a successful journey.

SECTION 1 ▶

WHERE ARE WE GOING?

Sometimes we take a journey based on the recommendation of others. We hear about a successful trip and we'd like to mirror the experience. Sometimes school leaders implement new approaches based on the success someone has heard about, read about, attended a conference about, or experienced in a previous role. We advocate the use of a model to help schools with the planning at this stage of the journey as we believe that models can serve as targets from which staff members can backward plan and from which they can learn. Through the analysis of a mature RTI model that serves as a guide and inspiration, schools will launch their efforts by responding to these questions:

▶ What are we already doing?

▶ Of what we're doing, what are we doing well?

▶ What are the gaps in our supports for students?

We recognize that presenting schools with the mature RTI model of another school, a school that has spent years refining and improving their processes, is both a blessing and a potential curse. Examining models is a blessing because it confirms for schools that it can be done—that schools can build capacity, collaborate professionally, focus curriculum, alter schedules, repurpose staff assignments, acquire resources, administer assessments, and analyze data to improve all students' learning. But models can provide an overwhelming negative sensation for some—a sense of gloom. Educators may feel that they lack the resources to build such a system. They worry that they are so far away from the practices represented in the model. They fear that they do not have the commitment or the expertise to successfully transform practices. They feel as though the model represents the *only* way in which an RTI-based system can be built.

We believe in the power of models and strongly encourage school leaders to avoid the pitfalls that can sidetrack staff members when they are presented with a model that might seem to be impossible to emulate. The truth is that *every* school can successfully ensure that all students learn at high levels. The liberating news is that there are many pathways toward this goal.

WHERE ARE WE AND WHAT ARE THE NEXT STEPS?

Every journey has a starting point, and in order to figure out where we need to go and to catalogue our journey, we need to know where we are right now. Every school has some method of supporting students in their academic, social, and behavioral growth. Before embarking on a new practice, it is important for educators to take a detailed look at what they are currently doing. A school's starting point can be established by using a data- and evidence-based self-analysis of that school's current realities and state of readiness. This "current status" report will help to reveal gaps and overlaps and initiate the collaborative approach that will be necessary to refine or overhaul current practices. Building and sustaining an RTI-driven system of supports involves multiple processes, including:

- ► Guiding staff through the change process, including discussions about why the change is necessary, what the change will involve, how the change will be supported, and how the success of the change will be measured.

- ► Reflecting upon and refining core Tier 1 instruction for both academics and behavior.

- ► Identifying students in need, and diagnosing the causes of their difficulties.

- ► Researching, acquiring, and gaining competency with intervention strategies and resources.

- ► Researching, acquiring, and gaining competency with tools for monitoring student progress.

- ► Developing systems for a cyclical problem-solving process.

Determining which of those elements have not yet been addressed, which have been initiated, which have been established, and which have been successful is the first step of the RTI Roadmap model.

At the start of any successful journey, several factors must be taken into consideration such as the mode of travel, the time required, and where the rest stops will be. Everyone wants to have a great trip. As a school embarks on a process of change, it's important to think about similar factors. Based on an analysis of questions such as "Where are we going?" and "Where are we now?" school leaders strategically select next steps to address the greatest areas of staff and student need.

Initiative fatigue is a very real condition in our experience. School teams that attempt to tackle too many challenges or attempt to implement practices too quickly can anticipate difficulties. A collaborative examination of the evidence from Sections 1 and 2 can help guide schools in their first steps, or in their next steps. There are several questions that can guide this examination:

- ► In what areas do our students need the most support?
- ► In what areas would our staff members benefit from more support?
- ► Which initiatives would most significantly benefit students and most impact multiple content areas and domains?
- ► For what initiatives are we most prepared, both in terms of culture and structures?

Determining in which direction to take the first steps of the journey is a critical decision for schools following the RTI Roadmap. Building in early "wins" ensures ongoing commitment to being part of the journey and energizes educators to tackle some of the bumps on the road.

HOW ARE WE GOING?

To help avoid the ubiquitous question "Are we there yet?" the most successful journey planners build in the capacity to "shift on the fly" by allowing time in the schedule to spend an extra night at a favorite stop or to stay longer at a meal to enjoy a unique dessert, and also to deal with flat tires and delayed flights. Successful school change requires similar check-ins and a similar capacity to adjust to unforeseen difficulties and opportunities. What is the "flight plan" we should follow to initiate, monitor, revise, and sustain RTI-based school improvement practices? Just as students sometimes experience difficulties with executive functioning skills such as planning, organization, and time management, school teams can become stalled or sidetracked in their improvement efforts if the initiative is not nurtured. By following a systematic plan, one that prompts staff members to check in on progress and one that anticipates pain points, school leaders can ensure success. Success will not be achieved without obstacles emerging along the way. Randy Pausch and Jeffrey Zaslow (2008) describe these obstacles or brick walls educators encounter along the path to change as tests "to determine how badly we want something" (p. 52). If the intent at the start of the initiative is to look for a reason why it won't work, brick walls will materialize. If the intent is to see the work through to successful completion because it's the right work, was co-created by all, and will positively impact student outcomes, those walls will only be temporary obstacles. When progress is transparently and frequently monitored, when evidence is analyzed and revisions are made, improvements to student learning can be achieved and sustained.

WHAT DOES
STUDENT EVIDENCE REVEAL?

If your journey involves driving the family car, you may become fixated on the instrument panel as a method to continuously monitor all of the functions of your car. You may then miss the invigorating scenery and wildlife that could be right outside your windshield. Clearly, you need to monitor fuel levels and speed but you also need to enjoy the ride. The odometer does not need your attention while you are driving. External accountability measures have caused some educators to become fixated on numbers without much meaning being attached to them. Educators sometimes get caught up in gathering data but do not convert it into evidence. We must face a paradox—we assess too much and yet we need more information—by rethinking data as evidence. Evidence, provided through formal and informal assessments, is the engine that drives education and RTI. But it has to be the right evidence gathered with the right tools.

What evidence formats do we need?

- ► Which students have significant gaps in the foundational prerequisite skills of literacy, numeracy, or behavior? We gather this information using *screeners.*

- ► To what extent are students learning the core content we are teaching during our initial, scaffolded, differentiated instruction? This evidence comes to us via *common formative assessments (CFAs).*

- ► What are the antecedents and/or the reasons that explain the difficulties of students who are at risk? *Diagnostics* are utilized to gather this information.

- ► To what extent are students responding to supplemental supports? We call this *progress monitoring* and use various methods to gather the feedback.

Evidence, when gathered accurately, analyzed collaboratively, and used to guide decisions, can motivate students and staff members to expect more from themselves and to persevere through the difficulties that will arise.

WHAT'S THE MOST IMPORTANT TIER?

Every successful journey has a "most important" aspect. Maybe it's the car you're driving, the extra legroom on the flight, or staying at a four-star resort instead of a three-star hotel. In education, and specifically in a well-defined RTI system, there is equally a most important aspect or hinge element—the piece that determines whether or not the work will lead to success. In RTI, this piece is the school's Tier 1 instruction and assessment practices. A standards-driven, well-defined, "unwrapped" Tier 1 informs all of RTI. A deep understanding of mapping, instruction, and assessment within academic and behavioral domains will ensure more students learn at a deeper level during core blocks of instruction. Without addressing equity and access in core programs; without focused, viable, and well-defined curricular units; without collaborative, cognitive planning, we will neither make significant gains in the number of students adequately responding to core instruction nor ensure all students learn at the levels of depth and complexity necessary to graduate from high school ready for college or a skilled career.

WHAT ARE THE CRITICAL STRUCTURES OF AN RTI MODEL?

Planning a successful journey involves knowing the priorities of everyone on the trip, the budget that is available, and the time that can be allotted. Educators looking to effect change in their schools also need to know who's with them and what skills those people have, and how much money and time there is to work with. Logistical questions related to school processes must be proactively addressed to ensure that the knowing-doing gap is closed:

- ► Which students and student needs require more attention?
- ► Which staff members are best positioned to provide supports?
- ► When will these supports be provided within the school day?

► Where will these supports be provided?

► What resources, strategies, and/or programs are necessary to meet diagnosed needs?

THE JOURNEY AWAITS

RTI involves an exciting and dramatic redesign of general and special education. Both need to change and the entire way in which we educate children requires our attention if schools are going to meet their lofty goals. Tweaking will not be sufficient. It is virtually impossible to list every intervention educators will need to meet the unique needs of every student. Each school will have local, contextual needs that will require local, contextual responses. This will require educators to combine the principles of RTI with new ways of thinking. School leaders will need to apply research and proven practices to meet the individual needs of their students using the distinct talents and resources of the professionals who serve those students. The RTI Roadmap that follows will assist in diagnosing a school's RTI needs—academic and behavioral—and in prescribing localized, contextualized solutions and potential next steps. The journey awaits!

SECTION 1 ►

WHERE ARE WE GOING?

To best plan for instruction, teacher teams "backward plan" from collaboratively created assessments. Similarly, we believe schools will be wise to begin their RTI journey by examining models of successful schools. These models represent what's possible when schools devote years to building robust systems of support, driven by the principles of RTI, that anticipate challenges and deliver instruction and intervention related to all student needs. Please remember: Models are not meant to be blindly replicated. They should not result in sentiments such as "We could never do this," or "We do not have the resources or personnel to do this," or "We would never get the buy-in to do this." Models are idea generators—samples of one school's solution. They are demonstrations that it is possible to build systematic sets of supports for students and that we as educators have the skill needed to do so. When we summon the will to take the *first* steps and to proceed to the *next* steps, all students grow and achieve the highest levels of success.

The notion of identifying the essential attributes of effective organizations is common both within education (Edmonds, 1979; Reeves, 2004; Lezotte, 1991; Marzano, Pickering, and Pollock, 2001; Marzano, 2003) and outside of education (Peters and Waterman, 1982; Collins and Porras, 1994; Collins, 2001). We have tried to make this practice of identifying the model attributes of organizations more relevant and accessible for educators by describing such attributes in the context of actual schools. In doing so, we have drawn upon our direct experiences leading schools and the experiences of our close colleagues, as well as research and literature from the field of RTI (Fuchs and Fuchs, 2006, 2007, 2008, and 2009; Buffum, Mattos, and

Weber, 2009, 2010, and 2012; Hierck, Coleman, and Weber, 2011; Hattie, 2009).

Before introducing the elementary model, there are a few necessary reminders about the robust, RTI-driven systems of support identified as tiers. Tiers are intended to define different intensities and types of support that students may require; support structures are classified in tiers, but students are not labeled, defined, or placed in tiers.

TIER 1

► Consists of a guaranteed and viable curriculum that will result in mastery (not just coverage) of essentials to the level of depth and complexity demanded of 21st-century learners.

► Features differentiated and scaffolded pedagogy and routines so that all students can access core content and engage meaningfully within their zones of proximal development.

► This guaranteed, viable curriculum includes both academic and behavioral domains.

TIER 2

► Supports for students that require more time and alternative strategies and approaches to master the content initially addressed within Tier 1.

► Involves gathering evidence about which students will require this support and with which skills they will need alternative strategies and approaches, as well as securing the time, personnel, and resources to respond.

► Is validated by researchers, including Benjamin Bloom (1968 and 1984), who demonstrated that an impressive

95 percent of students will achieve mastery of essential content with these Tier 2 supports as a companion to Tier 1 instruction, a model he named "mastery learning."

► Tier 2 supports (more time and alternative strategies and approaches to master Tier 1 essentials) can be applied to behavior as well as academic content.

TIER 3

► Supports for students who experience significant difficulties with any and all content because of significant deficits in their foundational literacy, numeracy, and behavior skills.

► Involves identifying these students and their areas of deficit early; identification need not be laborious; the process is typically known as universal screening.

► Involves providing intensive, targeted supports to begin closing gaps with a great sense of urgency; for example, each school year must end with educators having a solid understanding of students requiring Tier 3 supports and an emerging understanding of the antecedents of their struggles so that the next year's intensive interventions can begin the first week of school.

The goal of all students learning at high levels requires an all-hands-on-deck approach. *All* staff members—special education staff, general education staff, teaching staff, administrative staff, paraprofessional staff—must work together in creative and new ways to meet the needs of *all* students—students with Individualized Education Programs (IEPs), students meeting current grade-level expectations, students exceeding current grade-level expectations, students learning English as a second language, etc. Students must be supported based on their needs, not their labels. Staff members must support students based on their expertise and availability, not based on their current assignments or funding sources.

MODEL ELEMENTARY SCHOOL

We believe that response to instruction and intervention can be used synonymously and interchangeably with the very notion of schooling—of teaching and learning. Thus, our descriptions of fictional model schools will be fairly comprehensive. This section includes both graphic and narrative descriptions of the RTI-driven support systems of a diverse elementary school within a major U.S. city. More than 80 percent of students at this school are classified as English language learners and are eligible for free or reduced-price lunch.

RTI Grid

The table in Figure 1.1 summarizes the goals and actions of the model elementary school.

The RTI Engine

All school decisions are informed by *evidence*. Evidence is the engine of RTI. At all tiers of support and within each domain, evidence drives initial approaches and allows staff to define needs and target supports when students are not yet responding to instructional and intervention efforts.

The simple illustration in Figure 1.2 could be superimposed within each of the sections of the RTI Grid in Figure 1.1. Teacher teams use this process when designing, delivering, and differentiating supports to ensure that all students access and master essential content. RTI teams, composed of staff members who are engaged with

FIGURE 1.1	RTI Grid		
	Academics	**Social Behaviors**	**Academic Behaviors**
Tier 1	• Standards-driven curriculum maps • Instructional framework to continuously refine and improve instruction • Common formative assessments to provide the "target" and drive instruction	• School-wide (across grades and classrooms) common expectations that are consistently reinforced • Explicit teaching of desired behaviors • 5:1 ratio of positive acknowledgments to negative interactions	• Executive functioning and self-regulatory behaviors that support success with short-term and long-term academic tasks • These academic behaviors are both explicitly taught and consistently embedded within content-area instruction
Tier 2	• Specific times, schedules, and identified personnel to provide supports • Thirty minutes four times a week for reading and for mathematics • Grade-level schedules are staggered to maximize the use of support personnel • Supports involve more time and alternative approaches to ensure that students master the essentials • Evidence from common formative assessments and data analysis protocols drives these supports	• Simple diagnostic protocols to ensure that staff members know "what" behavior to target and "why" the student might be misbehaving • Identification and communication of the target behavior and matching strategy to teacher and student • "Check in/check out" process to mentor students and monitor the effectiveness of strategies • Focus on reteaching and more frequently reinforcing common expectations • For students with moderate, immediate deficits in behavioral skills	• Simple diagnostic protocols to ensure that educators develop an emerging and ever-increasing understanding of the antecedents of motivational and volitional needs • Identification and communication of the target behavior and matching strategy to teacher and student • "Check in/check out" process to mentor students and monitor the effectiveness of strategies • Focus is on reteaching and more frequently reinforcing common expectations • For students with moderate, immediate deficits in behavioral skills
Tier 3	• Students with deficits in foundational skills—who are not yet responding to instruction and intervention—receive intensive, 30-minute sessions of support in place of less essential content • The less essential content that students miss shifts every two weeks, with two weeks following an "A" schedule for interventions and the next two weeks following a "B" schedule **Programs:** • Math—Every Day Counts and Destination Math • Phonological Awareness—Earobics • Phonics—Intervention by Design • Fluency—Destination Reading • Comprehension—Soar to Success and Reading Advantage	• For students who are not responding to Tier 2 supports and/or have been diagnosed to have intensive needs in specific areas—anger, trauma, etc. • Using research-based interventions such as Anger Coping and CBITS in small groups or individually • These require specific programs, and programs require training	• For students who are not responding to Tier 2 supports and/or have been diagnosed to have intensive needs in specific areas—motivation, self-image, etc. • Using research-based approaches in attribution (Weiner, 2005) and self-efficacy (Bandura, 1977) • These require specific programs, and programs require training

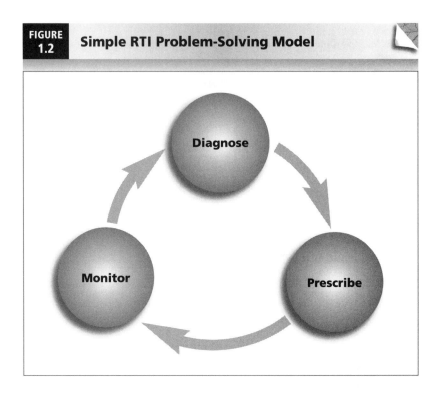

FIGURE 1.2 Simple RTI Problem-Solving Model

students and/or possess the diagnostic skills to help determine *why* a student is experiencing difficulties and *what* supports will best meet the diagnosed needs, meet every other week to problem-solve and determine appropriate supports.

Problem Solving and Assessment

The educators at this model elementary school have spent years refining their use of key assessments and evidence-gathering tools and processes, as well as their management, warehousing, organization, and use of data. Figure 1.3 lists assessments for each tier.

Formal data and evidence are gathered using the tools listed in Figure 1.3. More informal and qualitative—but equally significant—evidence is entered on a weekly basis into EduSoft. The exchange of

FIGURE 1.3	**Assessment for Each Tier**		
	Tier 1	**Tier 2**	**Tier 3**
CFAs	Every half-month in all content areas		
Screeners			• easyCBM™ for reading and mathematics • Student Risk Screening Scale (SRSS) and Student Internalizing Behavior Screening Scale (SIBSS) for behavior • Staff-to-staff electronic communication for all domains using EduSoft
Progress monitoring		• Alternate versions of portions of the common formative assessment • "Check in/check out" for behavior	• easyCBM™ for reading and math • "Check in/check out" or behavior intervention plan (BIP) for behavior
Diagnostics		• Diagnostic interviews in phonological awareness, phonics, fluency, vocabulary/comprehension, attention, motivation, early numeracy, and overall mathematics • BEAR (Basic Early Assessment of Reading) • Diagnostic Assessments of Reading for overall reading • Assistance from psychologist, speech and language pathologist, and occupational therapist for additional diagnostic supports • Scales of Independent Behavior—Revised for social and academic behaviors • Functional Behavioral Analysis (FBA) to inform the creation of BIPs	
Data organization	Data Director is used to warehouse data, record notes, and communicate with all internal stakeholders		

information and the problem-solving process are facilitated by the following meetings and processes:

▶ Teacher teams meet weekly to complete their established Data Team tasks and to discuss students they are especially concerned about. Notes on these students are entered into EduSoft by Friday afternoon.

▶ The RTI team (principal, psychologist, counselor, speech and language pathologist, specialists, and interventionists) meets twice a month to solve problems on behalf of students who have been identified as priorities by teacher teams and the RTI team. Priority students are those who have recently been identified as at-risk or those who are not adequately responding to the current levels of support. The notes from these meetings are entered into EduSoft for all internal stakeholders to review and act upon.

The key leader in the problem-solving and assessment process, and in the entire RTI-based system of support, is the principal. The principal drives the process, asking key questions, holding staff accountable, and ensuring that required resources are allocated.

A Guaranteed, Viable Curriculum in Academics and Behavior

Over the past several years, staff members in this school have designed and refined curriculum maps in all content areas. The maps represent the essential standards that all students must master within the school year and within each block of instruction. Maps have been refined as increased levels of vertical articulation have revealed gaps in content or student learning. Common formative assessments have been crafted that represent the level of rigor and the format at which students must demonstrate mastery. Because these assessments include tasks that require extended responses, the educators have crafted scoring guides, and they have selected anchor solutions from exemplary student work to guide the accurate grading and analysis of assessment results.

In the area of behavior, the school has adopted "respect, responsibility, and readiness" as the attributes on which instruction, reinforcement, and intervention focus. The educators have found that inattention and classroom disruption represent the greatest areas of student need. The school has adopted "motivation, metacognition, and monitoring" as key attributes of desired academic behaviors. They regularly support students in behaving in authentically engaged ways and in employing executive functioning skills (planning, organization, time management) when completing tasks, large and small.

Bell Schedule

The school's schedule was altered three years ago by inserting one 30-minute "intervention/enrichment" block once a week to provide Tier 2 supports to students in reading. Due to the positive impacts of these supports on student learning, the school now has a 30-minute intervention/enrichment block for Tier 2 reading and a 30-minute intervention/enrichment block for Tier 2 mathematics in the schedule four days a week. Students are dismissed one hour early each Wednesday, when educators collaborate and engage in professional development. Figures 1.4, 1.5, and 1.6 contain the school's schedules, including intervention blocks, for different grade levels.

Schedule for Kindergarten and First Grade

Time	Content
8:00–10:00	English language arts
10:05–10:20	Recess
10:25–11:25	Math
11:30–12:05	Lunch
12:10–12:40	Special/elective
12:45–1:15	Social studies
1:20–1:50	Science
1:55–2:25	Intervention/enrichment block 1
2:30–3:00	Intervention/enrichment block 2

FIGURE 1.5	Schedule for Second and Third Grade	

Time	Content
8:00–9:00	Math
9:05–9:35	Special/elective
9:40–9:55	Recess
10:00–12:00	English language arts
12:05–12:40	Lunch
12:45–1:15	Intervention/enrichment block 1
1:20–1:50	Intervention/enrichment block 2
1:55–2:25	Social studies
2:30–3:00	Science

FIGURE 1.6	Schedule for Fourth and Fifth Grade
Time	**Content**
8:00–8:30	Social studies
8:35–9:05	Science
9:10–10:10	Math
10:15–10:45	Special/elective
10:50–11:05	Recess
11:10–11:40	Intervention/enrichment block 1
11:45–12:15	Intervention/enrichment block 2
12:20–12:55	Lunch
1:00–3:00	English language arts

Students who require Tier 3 supports—who have been diagnosed to require intensive assistance with foundational skills—temporarily miss special classes, social studies, or science. The school leaders and educators believe that students with significant deficits in reading or mathematics require immediate, intensive, and targeted supports to at least get back on track for high school graduation, and to graduate ready for college or a skilled career. While students may miss time within these critical content areas temporarily, until they have gotten back on track to meet grade-level expectations, they need not miss the same content each week. The intervention schedule is shifted every two weeks, moving the time during which the Tier 3 support is provided, so that while students may miss attending a certain class, they will not miss that same class during the following two-week cycle. The compromise is imperfect, but illiteracy and innumeracy will not allow a student to access opportunities later if they are not intensively ameliorated early.

Intervention Schedule

Over the last several years, the school has inventoried the allocation of all human resources, attempting to ensure that personnel spend as much time providing direct supports to students as possible. This has resulted in repurposing classroom assistants and one member of the office staff. To help assistants work more efficiently, they now travel from classroom to classroom to provide targeted small-group supports to students; teachers have staggered the start times of their instructional blocks to allow this to occur (as is shown in Figures 1.4, 1.5, and 1.6). The office staff has been reduced from three to two members; the third member of the previous office staff was retrained to become an interventionist. The workload of the office was streamlined through technology, more efficient processes, and by shifting responsibilities among administrative and teaching staff. The school now utilizes four interventionists. These interventionists provide small-group supports during Tier 1 English language arts and mathematics instruction, Tier 2 supports during the intervention/enrichment block, and targeted Tier 3 supports to students most at risk. A week's roster for students requiring Tier 3 support is included in Figure 1.7, and a daily schedule for one of the interventionists is illustrated in Figure 1.8.

FIGURE 1.7   Roster for Tier 3 Supports

Interventionist Mrs. Harrison Phonological Awareness	Interventionist Mrs. Harrison Advanced Phonics	Interventionist Mrs. Harrison Advanced Phonics	Interventionist Mrs. Harrison Fluency
Jason (1st)	Angel (5th)	Juan (5th)	Brenda (5th)
Erin (Kinder)	Sergio (4th)	Christian (4th)	Anthony (4th)
Bella (1st)	Marisol (5th)	Brandon (4th)	Stephanie (5th)
Sadie (Kinder)	Dominique (4th)	Stephanie (5th)	Isabel (4th)
Anahi (Kinder)	Antonio (5th)	Brenda (5th)	Jocelyn (4th)
Summer (Kinder)	Daniel (5th)		

Interventionist Mrs. Barquer Phonological Awareness	Interventionist Mrs. Barquer Numeracy	Interventionist Mrs. Barquer Comprehension	Interventionist Mrs. Barquer Comprehension
Logan (1st)	Saul (5th)	Lupe (4th)	Saray (5th)
Abraham (1st)	Johnny (5th)	Lesley (5th)	Jerrylee (4th)
Marisol (1st)	Brittany (4th)	Maite (4th)	Amayrani (4th)
Zoe (1st)	Jennifer (5th)	Jesus (5th)	Kim (5th)
	Lexandra (4th)	Fabiola (4th)	Kevin (4th)
	Marleni (5th)		

Interventionist Mrs. Cooper Phonics	Interventionist Mrs. Cooper Phonics	Interventionist Mrs. Cooper Comprehension	Interventionist Mrs. Cooper Phonics
Saul (3rd)	Lupe (5th)	Eric (2nd)	Estefania (3rd)
Lucas (2nd)	Lesley (4th)	Daysi (3rd)	Alexis (4th)
Isaiah (3rd)	Daysi (5th)	Ian (3rd)	Natalie (3rd)
Blake (3rd)	Maite (5th)	Chance (2nd)	Francisco (3rd)
Brittany (2nd)	Jesus (5th)	Chase (3rd)	Elvis (4th)
Natalie (2nd)		Mark (3rd)	Anayeli (3rd)

Interventionist Mr. Gregory Phonics	Interventionist Mr. Gregory Numeracy	Interventionist Mr. Gregory Phonological Awareness/Early Phonics	Interventionist Mr. Gregory Fluency
Jason M (5th)	Fabiola (5th)	Juan (1st)	Jerrod (5th)
Anahi (4th)	Yareth (4th)	Christian (2nd)	Vanessa (4th)
German (5th)	Audrey (4th)	David (2nd)	Jorge (3rd)
Dulce (5th)	Shane (5th)	Stephanie (1st)	Ariana (4th)
Jason R (4th)	Lesley (4th)	Yareth (1st)	Jason (3rd)
Samantha (4th)		Ian (2nd)	Azucena (4th)
Omar (5th)			
Jasmine (4th)			

FIGURE 1.8 **Interventionist's Schedule**

Mrs. Harrison—Interventionist—Schedule			
Times	**Focus**	**Program**	**Location**
8:00–8:30	Tier 1 ELA—Mrs. Wilson (4th)		Room 123
8:30–9:00	Tier 1 ELA—Ms. Norgren (5th)		Room 125
9:00–9:30	Tier 1 ELA—Mr. Beyer (3rd)		Room 114
9:30–10:00	Phonics	Intervention by Design	Room 212
10:25–10:55	Tier 1 math—Mrs. Pedersen (2nd)		Room 105
10:55–11:25	Tier 1 math—Mrs. Marshall (3rd)		Room 116
11:30–12:00	Phonological Awareness	Earobics	Room 212
12:45–1:15	Phonological Awareness	Earobics	Room 212
1:20–1:50	Comprehension	Soar to Success	Room 212
1:55–2:25	Tier 2 ELA (2nd)		Room 105
2:30–3:00	Tier 2 math (2nd)		Room 105

MODEL
SECONDARY SCHOOL

Secondary schools can just as efficiently and effectively systemize supports for all students. More than 55 percent of students at a fictional model secondary school are classified as English language learners, and more than 45 percent are eligible for free or reduced-price meals.

RTI Grid

The grid in Figure 1.9 summarizes the goals and actions of this model secondary school.

FIGURE 1.9	RTI Grid		
	Academics	**Social Behaviors**	**Academic Behaviors**
Tier 1	• Standards-based curriculum maps for each course • Teacher-led "lesson studies" to inform improvements to pedagogy • Common formative assessments to provide the "target" and drive instruction • Cornell notes employed in all classrooms • Literacy and nonfiction writing across all content areas	• School-wide (across grades and classrooms) common expectations that are consistently reinforced and monitored by all staff in all settings • Explicit teaching of desired behaviors in all classrooms and reinforcement at critical times of the school year • 5:1 ratio of positive acknowledgments to negative interactions	• Executive functioning and self-regulatory behaviors that support success with short-term and long-term academic tasks • Academic behaviors are both explicitly taught and consistently embedded within content-area instruction • Academic behaviors are connected to the overarching expectations of the school

| FIGURE 1.9 | RTI Grid *(continued)* | | | |

	Academics	Social Behaviors	Academic Behaviors
Tier 2	• Specific times, schedules, and identified personnel to provide supports • Supports involve more time and alternative approaches to ensure that students master the essentials covered in the maps • Co-planned/co-taught courses • Academic center— specific teachers pull students for specific activities • Additional times for credit recovery • Targeted study sessions (after school, lunch, X block) focused on specific skill or content areas	• Simplified Functional Behavior Analyses (FBAs) to ensure we know "what" behavior we're targeting and "why" the student might be misbehaving • Identification and communication of selected strategy to teacher and student • "Check in/Check out" process to mentor student and monitor the effectiveness of strategy • For students with moderate, immediate skill deficits in behavioral skills • Offer replacement behavior as students work toward demonstrating the expected behavior	• Simplified Functional Behavior Analyses (FBAs) to ensure that we develop an emerging and ever-increasing understanding of the antecedents of students' motivation and volitional needs • Identification and communication of selected strategy to teacher and student • "Check in/Check out" to mentor student and monitor the effectiveness of strategy • The focus is on reteaching and more frequently reinforcing common expectations • Assess whether the deficit is competency-based or conduct-based
Tier 3	• Students with deficits in foundational skills—who are not yet responding to instruction and intervention—receive intensive 30-minute sessions during the second half of select periods, during noncore instruction, or during zero period from a highly qualified staff member • Support may require intensive one-on-one instruction for significant skill deficiency **Programs:** • Math—Concepts and Skills and Destination Math • Decoding—Destination Reading • Comprehension—Soar to Success and Reading Advantage • Fluency—Focus Forward and What's Happening	• For students who are not responding to Tier 2 supports and/or have been diagnosed to have intensive needs in specific areas—anger, trauma, etc. • Using research-based intervention such as Anger Coping and CBITS in small groups or individually • These require specific programs and may involve self-contained classrooms	• For students who are not responding to Tier 2 supports and/or have been diagnosed to have intensive needs in specific areas—motivation, self-image, etc. • Using research-based approach (Wraparound) to build constructive relationships and support networks • These require specific programs and may include pullout and additional support from special education personnel

The RTI Engine

The information gleaned from data and evidence again drives the simple problem-solving model that the school applies to each section of the RTI model (as shown in Figure 1.10). Teams use this process to design, deliver, and differentiate to ensure that all students access and master essential content.

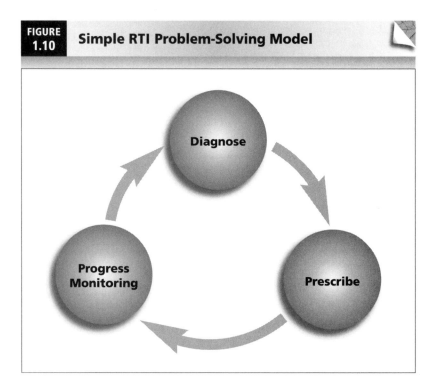

FIGURE 1.10   **Simple RTI Problem-Solving Model**

Problem Solving and Assessment

This model secondary school has refined its use of key assessments and evidence-gathering tools and processes, as well as its management, warehousing, organization, and use of data. Assessments for each tier are listed in Figure 1.11.

FIGURE 1.11	Assessment for Each Tier		
	Tier 1	**Tier 2**	**Tier 3**
CFAs	Every month in all content areas		
Screeners			• Promise Learning—Math • easyCBM™ for reading • Student Risk Screening Scale (SRSS) and Student Internalizing Behavior Screening Scale (SIBSS) for behavior • Staff-to-staff electronic communication for all domains using EduSoft
Progress monitoring		• Alternate versions of portions of the common formative assessment • "Check in/check out" for behavior	• easyCBM™ for reading and mathematics • "Check in/check out" for behavior
Diagnostics		• Diagnostic interviews in phonological awareness, phonics, fluency, vocabulary/comprehension, attention, motivation, early numeracy, and overall mathematics • Diagnostic Assessments of Reading for overall reading • Scales of Independent Behavior—Revised and Simplified Functional Behavioral Analysis for social and academic behaviors • Assistance from psychologist, speech and language pathologist, and occupational therapist for additional diagnostic supports	
Data organization	Data Director is used to warehouse data, record notes, and communicate with all internal stakeholders		

Formal data and evidence are gathered using the tools listed in Figure 1.11. More informal and qualitative evidence is entered on a weekly basis into EduSoft. The exchange of information and the problem-solving process are facilitated by the following meetings and processes:

> ▶ Teacher teams meet weekly to complete their established Data Team tasks and to discuss students they are especially concerned about. Notes on these students are entered into EduSoft by Friday afternoon.

> ▶ The RTI team (principal, assistant principals, psychologist, special education staff, counselor, speech and language pathologist, specialists, and interventionists) meets twice a month to discuss students who have been identified as priorities by teacher teams and the RTI team. Priority students are those who have recently been identified as at-risk or those who are not adequately responding to the current levels of support. A primary role of this team is to ensure that Tier 3 supports are targeted and effective.

The key leader in the problem-solving and assessment process, and in the entire RTI-based system of support, is the principal. The principal drives the process, asking key questions, holding educators accountable, and ensuring that required resources are allocated.

A Guaranteed, Viable Curriculum in Academics and Behavior

The staff members have designed and refined pacing calendars in all content areas over the past several years. The calendars represent the Priority Standards that should be mastered by all students within each course. They are not daily or delivery-method specific, but they do ensure sufficient time is provided to the learning progressions that educators know will be critical for success. Common formative assessments have been crafted that represent the level of rigor and format at which students must demonstrate mastery. Teams have crafted scoring guides, and they have selected exemplars to guide the accurate grading and analysis of assessment results.

In the area of social behaviors, the school has adopted "respect, responsibility, and pride" as the attributes on which instruction, reinforcement, and intervention focus. The school intentionally aligned its behavior expectations with its elementary school. School leaders and educators have found that engagement and defiance represent the greatest areas of student need. In the area of academic behaviors, the school has adopted "motivation, metacognition, and monitoring" as their key attributes to align with the expectations at their neighboring elementary school. They regularly support students in behaving in authentically engaged ways and in employing executive functioning skills when completing tasks, large and small.

Bell Schedule

This secondary school began three years ago by realigning its traditional secondary school block schedule by inserting a 25-minute intervention block into the schedule four days a week (Monday through Thursday) as part of an extended lunch to provide identified supports to students in mathematics and English language arts. For those students on track, this additional time is devoted to enrichment and extension of their learning. Additionally, on Friday the students arrive later and the school day begins with 55 minutes of staff collaboration time during which the educators meet in their professional learning communities to review and identify kids who might need additional support. Figure 1.12 illustrates the secondary school schedule.

Students who require Tier 3 supports—who have been diagnosed to require intensive assistance with foundational skills—temporarily miss class during electives, social studies, or science, or during "zero period." While zero period has traditionally been a time when ad-

FIGURE 1.12	Secondary Schedule		
Monday–Thursday		**Friday**	
Period 0	6:54–7:54	Collaboration	7:30–8:25
Period 1	8:00–8:50	Period 1	8:30–9:18
Period 2	8:56–9:50	Period 2	9:24–10:14
Break	9:50–10:05	Break	10:14–10:29
Period 3	10:11–11:01	Period 3	10:35–11:23
Period 4	11:07–11:57	Period 4	11:29–12:17
Lunch	11:57–12:58	Lunch	12:17–1:02
Interventions	12:03–12:28	Period 5	1:08–1:56
Period 5	1:04–1:54	Period 6	2:02–2:50
Period 6	2:00–2:50		

vanced students could take additional courses, Tier 3 interventions are now also offered. The school leaders and educators believe that students with significant deficits in reading or mathematics require immediate, intensive, and targeted supports to at least get back on track for high school graduation, and to graduate ready for college or a skilled career. The challenges that emerge in a secondary school are driven by inflexibility in restructuring students' classes. This places a premium on the interventions being imposed for a defined length of time to avoid frequent schedule changes for the student. Removing students from certain classes for short periods of time during which they can receive intense instruction/intervention in a required skill demands that educators "let go" of some structural beliefs. The compromise is imperfect, but the school recognizes that illiteracy and innumeracy will not allow a student to compete in the 21st-century workplace.

Intervention Schedule

Over the last several years, this school has inventoried the allocation of all human resources, attempting to ensure that personnel spend as much time providing direct support to students as possible. This has resulted in repurposing interventionists and support staff personnel. The interventionists provide 25-minute interventions to small groups during each block of the school schedule. By splitting the blocks in half, students only miss a portion of their noncore content electives. A typical daily roster for the interventionist to address students requiring support is included in Figure 1.13.

FIGURE 1.13	Interventionist's Schedule

Mr. Faulkner—Interventionist—Schedule			
Times	**Focus**	**Program**	**Location**
8:00–8:25	Tier 2 ELA		Room 123
8:25–8:50	Tier 2 ELA		Room 123
8:56–9:23	Tier 2 ELA		Room 123
9:23–9:50	Tier 2 ELA		Room 123
10:11–10:36	Tier 2 math		Room 123
11:07–11:32	Tier 2 math		Room 123
11:33–11:57	Decoding	Destination Reading	Room 123
12:03–12:27	Decoding	Destination Reading	Room 123
12:32–12:56	Fluency	Focus Forward	Room 123
1:01–1:25	Comprehension	Soar to Success	Room 123
1:30–1:54	Tier 3 math	Concepts and Skills and Destination Math	Room 123

SECTION 1
SUMMARY

Beginning with a goal in mind establishes a clear target that schools can aim for. Examining the journeys and successes of model schools can also be a motivating exercise. The next section will guide schools through a self-analysis and through the identification of first steps to developing an RTI-based system of supports. These actions are intended to facilitate a reflective process through which educators celebrate their successes, build on existing processes and practices, and identify initial tasks. Establishing the answers to such questions as "Where are we going?" "Where are we now?" and "What are the next steps?" is a critical and foundational step in school improvement efforts. Launching initiatives without knowing why changes are necessary, and without validating that successful change is feasible, can negatively impact school culture, imperil the success of the effort, and compromise the improvement of student learning. Providing a sense of hope built on acknowledging the skills and capacity of the adults working in schools today offers the best potential to transform traditional practices and achieve breakthroughs in student outcomes. We cannot afford to misstep. The stakes—student lives—are too high.

WHERE ARE WE AND WHAT ARE THE NEXT STEPS?

The next step in the journey begins with the RTI Roadmap Self-Analysis. Data, evidence, and artifacts gathered during the self-analysis will determine the first steps for schools and school systems as their leaders begin to systematize their efforts to meet all students' academic and behavioral needs.

The goal is college- and career-readiness for all students upon graduation from high school. To ensure that students achieve this ambition, we must not delay supporting students when we first identify their areas of need. These supports will best and most sustainably be provided through an RTI-based system.

The RTI Roadmap Self-Analysis is intended to determine a school's current realities and state of readiness. We recommend that schools invite an external critical friend to act as collaborative partner in this self-analysis. Members of the school staff should participate in the analysis, both because all staff members have knowledge of a school's current reality and because all staff members must be committed to and involved in the collaborative work to fully complete the self-analysis. Over the years, we've completed this data-gathering activity numerous times while helping schools determine strengths and areas for growth. Self-analysis requires courage, and this necessary step must not become a blame game and should not result in educators feeling overwhelmed—school staff members simply need to know where they are.

There are several options that schools may select from when collaboratively completing the self-analysis:

1. Individual staff members independently complete the self-analysis and then submit their responses to be collated and prepared for analysis.

2. Individual staff members independently complete the self-analysis and then collaborate with a team to discuss results before submitting team responses to be collated and prepared for analysis.

3. Teams collaboratively complete the self-analysis, then submit their responses to be collated and prepared for analysis.

4. The entire school meets to complete the self-analysis, then collates and analyzes responses.

There are also several options open to schools when analyzing the data, evidence, and artifacts from the self-analysis:

1. Internal expert team—Made up of representatives from key stakeholder groups, such as:
   - Administrative team
   - Department teams
   - Grade-level teams
   - Classified personnel
   - Clinicians

   This team analyzes data, evidence, and artifacts regarding RTI-related practices and prepares a synthesized report for the broader staff.

2. Internal expert groups—Mixed groups composed of stakeholders from various sections of the school, such as those listed in the "internal expert team" description, analyze data, evidence, and artifacts regarding RTI-related practices within specified RTI domains, such as:
   - Culture
   - Assessment
   - Data
   - Core instruction
   - Interventions

• Reading
• Mathematics
• Writing
• English language acquisition
• Behaviors
• Team meetings and communication
• Instructional schedules

They then prepare portions of a synthesized report for the entire staff.

3. Externally supported analysis—Experienced RTI experts collaborate with staff, guiding the analysis of data, evidence, and artifacts regarding RTI-related practices. The external team takes final responsibility for preparing a synthesized report for the school staff.

We share multiple options for engaging in this process to illustrate that while determining "where we are" is essential, school size and other logistical variables should be taken into consideration when determining how to best achieve that goal.

The purpose of the self-analysis is to inform decisions about the first or next steps that schools should pursue in their efforts to ensure that all students are on track to graduate ready for college or a skilled career. These next steps may involve efforts at improving school practices in:

▶ Culture and climate

▶ Reading domains

▶ Mathematics domains

▶ Writing domains

▶ Behavioral domains

The RTI Roadmap Self-Analysis (see Figure 2.1) is neither a checklist nor a "gotcha." Instead, the self-analysis includes statements of practice that we have helped create, or have observed, in schools

FIGURE 2.1 RTI Roadmap Self-Analysis

Rate your school from 1 to 4 on the criteria listed in the following table. Add any and all artifacts, documents, evidence, and data that support your analysis.

4: Consistent and effective
3: Fairly consistent and generally effective
2: Inconsistent and occasionally effective
1: Not present or observable

	Rate 1–4	Notes
Every staff member believes that all students can learn at very high levels.		
Staff members are willing to do whatever it takes (altering schedules, assignments, and past practices) to ensure that all students learn at the very highest levels.		
Instructional strategies are identified and shared that best help students master essential learning outcomes.		
The school clearly identifies and articulates, consistently models, and positively reinforces the *social* behaviors that it expects all students to exhibit, including but not limited to the areas of: ☐ Cooperation ☐ Attention ☐ Respect (physical and verbal) ☐ Attendance		
The school has clearly identified and articulated, consistently models, and positively reinforces the *academic* behaviors that it expects all students to exhibit, including but not limited to the areas of: ☐ Motivation ☐ Organization ☐ Study skills ☐ Task completion ☐ Emotional stability		
Every staff member at the school consistently models, corrects, and positively reinforces the *social* and *academic* behaviors that they expect all students to exhibit.		
School RTI teams and Data Teams use evidence on a regular basis to determine which students need additional time and support, the areas in which these identified students most need the additional time and support, and areas in which all students will benefit from additional time and support.		

FIGURE 2.1	RTI Roadmap Self-Analysis *(continued)*		
		Rate 1–4	**Notes**
An increasing percentage of all class assessments administered collaboratively are used formatively with students, and are used to collectively inform teaching and learning. They include: ☐ Pretests that assess the prerequisite skills that students should possess to successfully learn upcoming content and/or the students' knowledge of upcoming content. ☐ Mid-unit tests that assess student progress part of the way through a unit, but well before the end of the unit, so that timely interventions can be provided. ☐ End-of-unit tests that allow teams to know which students will continue to require support in mastering certain essential learning outcomes even though a new unit of instruction is set to begin. ☐ Formal or informal checks for understanding, including "tickets-out-the-door" and mid-lesson whiteboard checks within lessons. ☐ Progress monitoring that more frequently and validly monitors students' response to intervention, and, when errors are analyzed, can also diagnose students' needs.		
The school has built times into the instructional day for students to receive supplemental Tier 2 support *in addition to* Tier 1 (core) instruction *and* differentiated instruction provided by grade-level and content-alike teams.		
The school has inventoried all staff members' availabilities and abilities and has assigned them to directly providing supports to students, with initial and ongoing professional development provided. Teams meet regularly to coordinate their efforts on behalf of students. Processes ensure that information is efficiently documented and communicated to all stakeholders.		

throughout North America in which high levels of commitment to and success at improving student learning have been achieved, including staff practices or systems that schools create, employ, and sustain to support student needs (Buffum, Mattos, and Weber, 2009, 2010, and 2012; Hierck, Coleman, and Weber, 2011). It is essential that school leaders and educators not become discouraged when completing this self-analysis, when implementing structures related to RTI, or when doing any work associated with improving the educational opportunities for all students. We've been there! We've led continuous improvement efforts and continue to do so. Remember: There is more than one route that will get you to the desired destination; we aim to guide you, no matter what route you choose. All any group of educators can do is start where they are and take the next steps toward a more complete and successful system of supports for students. Do not beat yourselves up about how far you have to go ... and don't expect everything to happen immediately or all at once. Lastly, resist the urge to tackle multiple new initiatives; choose wisely, do it well, and you can expect your well-chosen and well-implemented effort to have a dramatic impact on student learning.

Please note that the self-analysis addresses more than what the professionals in schools *do*. Educators are also prompted to analyze what they *believe*. Successful RTI programs and high-performing schools are based on more than structures—they are based on cultures of high expectations and high levels of commitment.

Analysis must be followed by actions. The information gleaned from the analyses in Section 1: Where Are We Going? and earlier in this section help school leaders and educators identify the critical elements of RTI and lay the foundation for the RTI Roadmap. Educators must select and define the next (or the first) steps of the journey. This will require deep, meaningful collaboration to ensure that the most realistic and optimally powerful steps are chosen—collaboration that goes beyond being in the same room at the same time, beyond voting for the best choice, and beyond establishing a checklist of things to do—the type of collaboration that includes courage, trust, and crucial conversations and a shift in focus from "my students" to "our students." By embarking on this journey you are not simply determining a checklist of action steps; you are building a common language to define the direction in which your school is heading, and the checkpoints that you are attempting to reach along the way.

GREATEST AREAS OF NEED

The information gathered thus far will allow schools to identify their greatest areas of need. Analysis of multiple data sources can lead school teams to the identification and development of focused, high-priority, high-leverage solutions. Having dependable data sources is critical. It's not good enough to evaluate reading by counting the number of books taken from the library; an assessment of comprehension would yield better information. It is equally important that the analysis includes identifying staff needs. In order for teachers to become more strategic in their instructional decisions, the identification of gaps in their capacity to differentiate to meet the needs of all learners might need to be addressed.

The notion that focusing on the greatest areas of need yields results is linked to the Pareto Principle, which suggests that identifying and addressing the key elements impeding progress will result in the greatest impact. Ultimately this allows for the most efficient use of our time and resources. The Pareto Principle is derived from the notion that there are generally a few underlying causes that explain the majority of an organization's difficulties. It's often referred to as the 80:20 rule, suggesting that 80 percent of our challenges can be addressed by focusing on 20 percent of the causes. The analysis of those areas that are challenging can be very situational, requiring an in-depth, school-by-school analysis. There is no one-size-fits-all solution.

THE THREE GAPS

Conzemius and Morganti-Fisher (2012) suggest that identifying the greatest areas of need and the resultant priorities to address them can best be achieved by analyzing three gaps:

1. The accountability gap—The difference between today's performance and the performance to which we will be held accountable at some point in the future. How this future accountability level will be determined has the potential to create some angst for staff and derail the progress being made. This can neither be an arbitrary number arrived at as part of an assumed ongoing growth model (we just add one percent to last year's results, ignoring the students in class today and their relative scores) nor can it be so lax that it does not require much work to achieve. It's best arrived at in a fulsome, data-driven dialogue that looks at numerous factors impacting achievement results.

2. The proficiency gap—The difference between where we are today and 100 percent of students learning at a rate that enables them to graduate ready for college or a skilled career. We often hear that it is unrealistic to ever expect 100 percent of our students to master key content. While only a few sites can claim this success (and with a diverse student population), we maintain that this must be the objective. Put another way: Are you willing to identify those students to whom we ought not offer our best—to cut our losses by not adding to their skill set so that they are prepared for their transition to life beyond public school?

3. The change-over-time gap—The difference between our baseline performance data and where we are today in terms of student proficiency. This suggests that a student's current proficiency levels are measured against an initial baseline assessment to see if instruction has had a positive or negative

impact over time. This also provides some insight as to whether or not an intervention is having an impact and is worth continuing.

Conzemius and Morganti-Fisher (2012) suggest that the first gap is the one most often pursued by schools and districts and satisfies a compliance need. The second gap addresses the oft-stated goal of all students achieving proficiency, and they refer to this as the "commitment gap." The third gap gives some indication about the effectiveness of existing practices, and may predict future outcomes.

Analyzing these three gaps will assist school leaders and educators when identifying their greatest areas of need and when determining which high-impact, research-based practices will produce the highest gains. For example, at an elementary school, an intensive focus on core and supplemental reading supports might have the greatest impact, while at a secondary school, an intensive focus on core and supplemental behavioral supports might lead to the most dramatic and immediate increases in student achievement. Here again, the Pareto Principle rings true. Imagine the improvement in results that occurs when we have addressed those areas that represent the biggest gaps in student learning throughout the school. The improvement in schools will not happen because our most able students improve their already impressive results by a percentage point or two. It will come from closing the gap for our struggling students and moving all students forward in pursuit of the goal that 100 percent of students should be learning at the level of depth required to go on to college or a skilled career.

MOVING FROM GREATEST AREAS OF NEED TO GOALS

Collaboratively identifying the greatest areas of need for students and staff will allow for the development of high-leverage goals that will have a direct impact on student outcomes and, by extension, on the other areas of concern that are of a lower priority but still relevant.

Conzemius and Morganti-Fisher (2012) offer a strategy they refer to as "zone analysis" to help move the process from need-identification to action. The strategy involves disaggregating data sources to isolate where improvement is needed and matching the strategies that will best address these gaps. "Without this kind of analysis, all student performance remains lumped into an average, which tells us little about individual student performance and provides almost no guidance on what to do about it" (p. 52).

Schools must also distinguish between goals aligned with results and goals that merely indicate good intentions. We are in the results business, and have a responsibility to ensure that students make at least one year's worth of growth on their journey toward graduating high school prepared to continue to learn, whether in college or a skilled career. Goals that stop at changing processes but don't impact results drain away human and material resources and have the potential to create frustration. A sentiment often attributed to French writer Antoine de Saint-Exupery expresses this idea best: "A goal without a plan is just a wish." Being intentional about our goals will provide the clarity needed. You might start with a goal that says, "We will implement direct instruction (instruction that emphasizes a step-by-step approach while focusing on the essential learning) in mathematics." This may ensure a better process for delivering math content but may not impact student learning. By adding, "so that all students are able to master the most highly prioritized standards at grade level as measured by common formative assessments," adds the results focus needed. Within this goal you can also layer in research-based strategies for any sub-groups of students for whom the gaps may be larger, to ensure that those gaps are closed.

TAKING THE NEXT STEPS

Moving from the talk about next steps to the action of next steps requires just that—movement. Based on analyses, what information has emerged? What are your top three next steps? Your greatest areas of need? Consolidating the work of the first two sections may seem overwhelming, and schools often get stuck here. The temptation to "do it all at once" is strong, particularly when faced with external pressures that demand change in a short period of time. Remember the Pareto Principle and the notion that focusing intensely on a small number of items (twenty percent) will address a large portion (eighty percent) of the challenges. How, then, do you figure out which goals are most important? Our strident belief that behavior and academics are inextricably linked leads to the establishment of goals that impact both of these areas in our work with schools. Identifying your top three challenges and then engaging all educators at your site in a planning framework will ensure that the necessary focus and required resources are brought to the work.

As you examined the model schools outlined, did you see similarities to challenges you are facing? This may help identify your first or next steps when analyzing challenges and discussing methods of addressing them over time. Continuing to devote staff meeting time, collaboration time, and professional development time to addressing challenges and making midcourse corrections will help you achieve your desired outcomes. As you talk about the model schools, also celebrate your successes and look to leverage those as you continue the work. Figure 2.2 summarizes what needs to happen during the second section of your journey.

The template in Figure 2.2 will help schools identify their greatest areas of need and first and next steps. Carefully and collaboratively complete this important work; you will be using the results as you proceed through the RTI Roadmap.

FIGURE 2.2	**Determining Greatest Areas of Need**

Use this scoring to determine relative priorities when establishing your greatest areas of need. Remember the Pareto Principle to ensure proper focus and maximum impact.

4: Absolutely needed to improve student outcomes
3: Will have an impact but should not be a first step
2: Could be part of a future plan if data indicate
1: Not required at this time (or may be impacted by focus on other items)

From the RTI Roadmap Self-Analysis at the beginning of this section (Figure 2.1), our team generated the following list:	New Rating (1–4)	Identify each item listed as Academic (A), Social Behaviors (SB), or Academic Behaviors (AB)
1.		
2.		
3.		
4.		
5.		
6.		
7.		
8.		
9.		
10.		
11.		

FIGURE 2.2	Determining Greatest Areas of Need *(continued)*

Zone Analysis—The following data sources will be used to help identify our top three greatest areas of need:

1. Academic results from classrooms
2. Academic results from external assessments
3. Behavior data
4.
5.

The model school information in Section 1 highlighted these areas for us to consider/explore further:

1.
2.
3.
4.
5.

As a result of the analysis above, our goals for the next school year are:
(Note: There should be no more than three goals, and some schools may not have three)

1.
2.
3.

SECTION 2
SUMMARY

The first step in the journey toward high levels of learning for all students—a journey that we suggest is best completed within a Response to Intervention framework—is for schools to determine their current location. As educators reflect upon their school's strengths and identify areas where growth is needed, they can more accurately determine next steps. Evidence-based reflections can structure staff members' courageous conversations.

These courageous conversations are part of the larger—and critically important—topic of school culture. Culture will ultimately be the reason why a school succeeds in guaranteeing that all students will graduate from high school ready for college or a skilled career, or, alternatively, why school leaders struggle to get improvement efforts started or fail to sustain systematic improvement efforts. Determining a school's current reality has to do with identifying both what educators do and what they believe—about students and about themselves.

The Pareto Principle is a blessing and a welcome reminder for schools. Tackling too many areas of improvement will result in initiative fatigue—when attempting to implement several improvement efforts, schools may instead fail to implement any of the initiatives completely.

By carefully, collaboratively, and analytically examining the evidence from Sections 1 and 2, schools can ensure that their plans for first or next steps are likely to result in improving their systematic supports and increasing the achievement of all students. There will be a temptation to address any and all needs, but it is essential that school leaders resist that temptation. Focus is critical. If you commit to improving student outcomes in carefully selected, specific goal areas, you can expect student growth in many other areas to also improve.

Knowing what to do is nice—but actually doing it is necessary to impact student learning. The next section will describe the steps that schools can take to ensure that good ideas and best intentions translate into high levels of student achievement.

HOW ARE WE GOING?

Once schools have examined mature and successful RTI-based school models, analyzed their current levels of proficiency as related to Response to Intervention, and identified greatest areas of need and highest-leverage solutions, schools must initiate, monitor, revise, and sustain their RTI-based school improvement practices.

When organizations do not determine how they will know if they have successfully reached a goal or when they have successfully reached a goal—or specific areas in which success has been achieved and others in which midcourse corrections are necessary—there are several potential unfortunate outcomes:

► Pushback from less-than-enthusiastic stakeholders may undermine, or advocate terminating, improvement efforts.

► Less-than-optimally-successful areas will not receive the supports required to get them back on track.

► Particularly successful areas will not be identified, celebrated, and replicated.

► The appropriate time to initiate next steps will not be recognized.

School leaders and educators must identify measureable goals. They must define the variables that will be monitored. They must gather and analyze evidence. They must communicate analyses to stakeholders to adjust efforts and motivate the continuous drive to maximize student learning.

And, the school staff must be led. The principal and the administrative leadership team must meet regularly to ensure that efforts are coordinated and that information is communicated. Strong leadership is an absolute foundational prerequisite to successful RTI implementation. Principals and other leaders need not have all the answers, but they must ask all the questions and, with patient persistence, ensure that all staff members are working together toward the goal.

Success breeds success. Students will be more motivated to learn when they observe the growth achieved through their hard work. Educators will respond in the same way. We have found that even initially reluctant staff will develop a firmer commitment to new ideas when they witness or experience success. To maximize the chances of this occurring, schools must have systems that establish goals, measure progress toward those goals, and communicate those goals. Most schools can initiate RTI-based practices, but only schools that have a plan for sustaining these practices will optimize success and student learning. Figure 3.1 outlines the steps toward success.

We draw upon the work of Peter Senge (1990) and Michael Fullan (2010) in crafting a systems approach to this work. The work is too important and the required change too complex to proceed on our journey without signposts on the RTI Roadmap. Think of the Steps to Success listed in Figure 3.1 and explained on the following pages as executive functioning guidelines for schools. The steps represent a method for ensuring that the implementation process successfully leads to improved staff performance and student learning.

STEP 1. Clearly define the desired outcomes and establish completion dates.

At this stage of the journey toward RTI implementation, school leaders and educators are preparing to initiate their RTI-based practices. The first step is to clearly define the desired outcomes and establish completion dates. We recommend that educators set ambitious goals, known to some as Big Hairy Audacious Goals, or BHAGs (Collins, 2001). Each goal must be accompanied by reasonable target dates. These desired outcomes should not simply define what changes will

FIGURE 3.1 **Steps to Success for RTI-Based Practice**

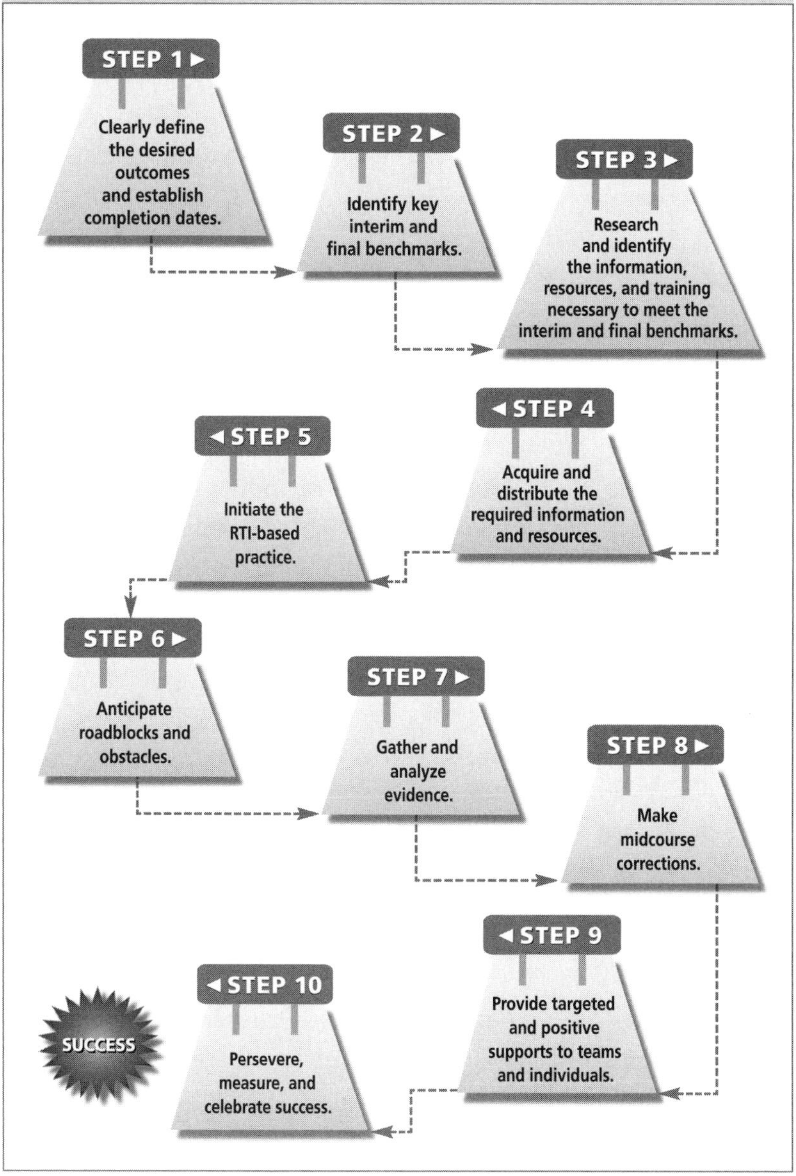

STEP 1 ►
Clearly define the desired outcomes and establish completion dates.

STEP 2 ►
Identify key interim and final benchmarks.

STEP 3 ►
Research and identify the information, resources, and training necessary to meet the interim and final benchmarks.

◄ STEP 4
Acquire and distribute the required information and resources.

◄ STEP 5
Initiate the RTI-based practice.

STEP 6 ►
Anticipate roadblocks and obstacles.

STEP 7 ►
Gather and analyze evidence.

STEP 8 ►
Make midcourse corrections.

◄ STEP 9
Provide targeted and positive supports to teams and individuals.

◄ STEP 10
Persevere, measure, and celebrate success.

SUCCESS

be made, or processes introduced, by staff; they must also define the measureable outcomes that will be achieved.

As is the case when creating the common formative assessments from which teachers will "backward plan" to drive instructional practice, educators must begin with the end goal of RTI-based improvement efforts in mind in order to define and drive professional practice. And, leaders must courageously and confidently communicate these goals to stakeholders.

STEP 2. Identify key interim and final benchmarks.

The next step is to identify key interim and final benchmarks. The goal in Step 1 is more global; in Step 2, educators must specify the outcomes that will serve as evidence of achieving the BHAGs.

Since the efficacy of interventions will always be determined through targeted progress monitoring of individual students' responses to those interventions, educators should consider other methods of benchmarking success. They should ask a question such as, "What improvements would occur as a result of our successful implementation of this RTI-based practice?" Examples of quantifiable outcomes include:

▸ Improved performance on common formative assessments.

▸ Improved completion rates on classwork and homework.

▸ Improved attendance rates.

Educators can also quantify more "qualitative" evidence that can be self-reported by students, as well as monitored by staff and parents, such as:

▸ Demonstration of pro-social behaviors such as cooperation and self-control.

▸ Rates of participation or other forms of engagement.

▸ Frequency of positive adult-to-student and student-to-student interactions.

These data can and should be gathered for both at-risk students and the overall student population.

"What gets measured gets done," a saying often attributed to author and management consultant Peter Drucker, rings true in schools. Gathering information can both motivate and inform.

STEP 3. Research and identify the information, resources, and training necessary to meet the interim and final benchmarks.

Educators must next research and identify the information, resources, and training necessary to meet those interim and final benchmarks. Staff members should find research and literature about the highest-leverage solutions for their greatest areas of need, as well as examples of schools and settings in which these solutions have thrived.

While we do not believe that purchasable programs are mandatory, and can in fact often distract or sidetrack well-intentioned efforts, materials and resources that meet the school's needs and plans should be researched. Lastly, school leaders must identify which professional development from outside experts is required and worthwhile, and which professional development staff members can conduct on their own. Educators can be cynical regarding professional development, but that cynicism usually reflects the quality, ongoing support, and actual implementation associated with the training they have experienced in the past; it does not negate the absolute need for professional development to continually enhance educators' capacities.

STEP 4. Acquire and distribute the required information and resources.

The identification of needed information, resources, and professional development is not enough. School leaders must next interact with members of the support staff at the school and district office who will perform the critical tasks of finding the best price, processing paperwork in a timely manner, and scheduling the delivery of materials.

The acquisition and distribution of the required information and materials is too often an undervalued step. We have worked in and with schools whose efforts have been stalled because the programs were found to be prohibitively expensive (often because the incorrect products were recommended for purchase or more products or materials than necessary were recommended for purchase), or because program materials have not arrived by the predetermined and planned launch date, or because professional development cannot be scheduled (trainers are not available or substitute teachers cannot be secured).

Communication is always the key, and there is simply no such thing as *too much* communication. We recommend that school leaders devote ample time to meeting face-to-face with support staff members from purchasing, finance, and distribution divisions so that they are part of the team, and so that they understand the school's mission and adopt the same sense of urgency about the necessity of all students learning at high levels that is expected of the educators in the school.

STEP 5. Initiate the RTI-based practice.

At some point, we must begin. Despite the fact that educators may not feel ready, and think that there is more that could be done to prepare, the RTI-based practice must be initiated. We recommend that school leaders be transparent about the fact that everyone involved will learn while doing. Action research, a hallmark of effective professional learning communities, is based on a ready-fire-aim philosophy. This is not to suggest that we are irresponsible, but rather that every day that we delay is a day that students are not benefiting from the potential of our change efforts.

So, having accomplished Steps 1–4, it is time to set a launch date and commit to revisit and revise the plan as data become available, a process described in subsequent steps. Launching any initiative, including RTI-based practices, will always benefit from specific habits.

First, leaders must follow through with teams and with individuals within the school. Staff members must feel supported, and they must feel as though the initiative, now launched, will be supported. Building individual and collective capacities can enhance this sense of feeling supported. Specifically speaking, professional development cannot end once the RTI-based practice begins; both educators and school leaders must continue to learn, through both formal (afterschool, half-day, and full-day training) and informal (one-on-one conversations, asynchronous electronic dialogues, book or article studies) venues.

It is also important to engineer early victories. This is not to suggest that leaders engage in chicanery. Instead, identifying immediate and positive results shows that it's possible to be successful right away when implementing an initiative. Early victories are motivating for every single stakeholder involved, so it's important for leaders to capitalize on opportunities to celebrate early successes, and communicate positive results widely.

Finally, upon initiating the planned RTI-based practice, all stakeholders must commit to revisiting the vision. Leaders on campuses must readdress the "why, what, and how" of the change. Why did we agree that these efforts are necessary? What behaviors and actions are necessary to meet our goals? How are we going to measure our successes? Staff members are predictably and understandably going to raise these questions. Leaders must proactively revisit them.

STEP 6. Anticipate roadblocks and obstacles.

Roadblocks and obstacles will certainly arise, so it's important to be prepared for them. Try to predict, from research of others' experiences, what these challenges may be and collectively acknowledge that roadblocks and obstacles are inevitable. Successfully persevering through predictable challenges will separate success from frustration.

One way to gain the upper hand on the next obstacle is to frequently check in with one another. Principals and other school leaders must get out of the office, ask questions, make observations, gauge the school's climate, and examine early evidence to be in a position to proactively address a challenge.

There are several other ways to prepare for roadblocks. Fiscal resources should be set aside to support the additional materials or professional development that may be required. Time should be set aside to have "town-hall-style" meetings to discuss challenges and solutions. Lastly, leadership teams should make checking in on the success of the change a priority during meetings.

Difficulties will emerge. Maintaining a patient persistence while managing stress is a key role in the RTI-based change practice for school leaders, and for the entire staff. The most precious of resources is time. If and when possible, give staff members the gift of time to collaborate, reflect, and recharge.

STEP 7. Gather and analyze evidence.

In Step 2, the key interim and final benchmarks were identified. For example, a school with a goal of improving students' oral reading fluency may establish a final benchmark of 100 percent of students scoring at the "benchmark" and "strategic" levels, with no students scoring at the "intensive" level. Given that 40 percent of students were scoring at the "intensive" level mid-year, and given that there are four months remaining in the year, a goal is set that the percentage of students scoring at the "intensive" level will be reduced by 10 points each month.

In Step 7, then, school teams gather and analyze evidence related to students' oral reading fluency rates, and share results with all staff each month. Analyses of results for groups of students with higher and lower relative rates of growth, as well as for individual students with higher and lower relative rates of growth, are conducted. We recommend that school leaders establish certain interim check-ins as key decision points. For example, while oral reading fluency rates are gathered, reported, and analyzed every month, the school staff may commit to analyzing data for the purpose of making decisions about resource reallocation and about which students and grade levels may require additional supports at three-month intervals. Change will be embraced and sustained if educators know that the success of the school's efforts will be measured and acted upon in a timely and direct manner.

STEP 8. Make midcourse corrections.

The purpose of gathering and analyzing evidence of the success of RTI-based practices is to enable educators to make midcourse corrections. Too many school teams conduct analyses without the willingness to make adjustments. Such decisions require courage; when evidence suggests that current efforts are not resulting in adequate levels of improvement, educators must boldly revise the plan. Such decisions also require prudence; we are not suggesting plans be abandoned altogether. The "why" that originally justified the change remains the same; minor shifts in the "what" and "how" may be necessary to increase the rates at which improvements are occurring. The proverbial baby should not be thrown out with the bath water.

Teams of educators can help prepare for the success of midcourse corrections by brainstorming possible scenarios in advance. What adjustments will need to be made if certain grade levels or content areas require more support? What adjustments will need to be made if success is reached sooner than expected? The key, as is so often the case, is a willingness and capacity to respond flexibly. It is essential to plan on making shifts in priorities when interim benchmark targets have not been reached. Such transitions may involve reprioritizing supports and resources and should not be delayed.

STEP 9. Provide targeted and positive supports to teams and individuals.

Conflict is inevitable when making significant changes in education. Conflict can be a productive experience, and may even be a requirement of substantive, transformational improvement. Evidence-informed midcourse corrections may involve providing targeted and positive supports to teams and individuals and may require crucial conversations.

When analysis of data associated with RTI-based practices reveals a need, leaders must exercise the courage to open a true dialogue. Students and staff members deserve leaders' best efforts, which means that leaders must proactively address shortfalls and develop an action plan. Such dialogues must not be punitive or evaluative. The goal is to continuously improve, and this goal applies to all stakeholders. We should start by assuming the best of intentions in our colleagues. Leaders should anticipate defensiveness and should consider that a cynic may simply be a frustrated idealist; the more cynical one seems, the more idealistic one likely used to be. Discover that idealism and find common ground and mutual purpose. Once consensus on an RTI-based practice to improve student learning is reached, participation is mandatory.

Targeted and positive supports may involve and necessitate more professional development, more individualized attention, and/or more material resources. Or, a more direct conversation may be required. Positive, proactive, and direct conversations must be a part of the journey. It's possible that a clarification of what is, and what is not, expected of staff must occur. Difficulties and disagreements, in our experience, sometimes occur because participants were unclear about what was expected. For example, a teacher feels that the curriculum maps dictate what must be done on a daily basis, when in fact they only define what students must know and be able to do by the end of the unit. Or, consensus on instruction that involves a gradual release of responsibility is interpreted to signify expectations for rigid instructional techniques. Clarifying what is and is not expected can often resolve confusion and improve teacher practices and student learning.

When more extensive conversations are required, a safe environment for honest dialogue is critical. School principals should ideally meet in their colleagues' space (such as a classroom), not in the principal's office. When meeting in the principal's office is the best option, sit with colleagues; do not face off from behind a desk. Another way of creating safety and building trust is to share the topic that will be discussed prior to meeting, allowing colleagues to prepare and avoid surprises. Start the dialogue by sharing your thought processes that have led to the conversation, and using facts (data, evidence, and research related to the RTI-based practice). We are increasingly fortunate in education to have a wealth of information, of facts, related to best practices (Hattie, 2009). The job of teaching children is too important for us to base decisions on opinions, hunches, or intuitions that are not based on research and evidence. Encourage colleagues to share their own facts and thought processes. Agree upon a next step, one that meets the identified need and one for which specific staff members can receive immediate supports. Timely, positive follow-up is another way of building trust. Educators need to know that their leaders will follow through on commitments.

Make sure everyone in the school knows that evidence-based practices can result in improvement in student learning and behavior. All students are capable of learning; it is educators who are the variable, and our actions and behaviors will make the difference.

STEP 10. Persevere, measure, and celebrate success.

Interim benchmarks are established so that midcourse corrections can be made. Final benchmarks are established so that we can determine that we have met our goals.

There will always be new challenges in education, a profession in which continuous improvement is a necessary reality for staff and students, so it is essential that successes be validated and celebrated. Reflection should also take place. What attributes of the RTI-based practice contributed to success? What revisions should be made in the future to proactively anticipate roadblocks and obstacles? What deficits in student learning and staff knowledge may have emerged in the endeavor that can inform our next RTI-based practice?

Step 10 involves leading and managing the entire process of change—the entire RTI-based practice. It also involves transitioning from one critical practice to another. When determining RTI needs, as described in Sections 1–3, school leaders will wisely identify a very limited number of initiatives on which to focus in order to maximize success and the impact on student performance. But after successfully meeting final benchmarks, it is likely that teams will transition to another area of focus.

The structures required for successful implementation and change can effectively be organized using the processes and structures described in this section. But in the end, culture will be more important, and cultural missteps will be a greater threat to success than structures. If it's predictable, it's preventable. We can predict that cultural obstacles will emerge. We can predict that some of our committed colleagues will experience frustrations. The following pages describe likely areas of frustration and how school leaders can respond.

THE "TIGHT-LOOSE" DEBATE

One likely pressure point for staff members in any change process is the "tight-loose" debate, which must be addressed, defined, and revisited. School leaders must define which expectations associated with school practices are "tight," or nonnegotiable, and which are appropriately "loose," or negotiable. It is impossible and unproductive, for educators and for students, for everything to be tight. It is equally inappropriate for everything to be loose. A clear understanding of what is nonnegotiable, and why, is absolutely critical.

For example, a sound Tier 1 program, whether in the domain of academics or behavior, is required to achieve a guaranteed, viable curriculum. We believe that rigid pacing guides inhibit flexibility and opportunities to differentiate. Flexible pacing guides, driven by prioritized standards that students must learn within a commonly taught unit with student learning measured by common formative assessments, are necessary.

BEHAVIOR INSTRUCTION

Another predictable area in which school leaders may experience pushback from internal stakeholders is in the area of teaching students to behave. Some educators do not believe it is their responsibility to teach the behaviors that students must display while at school, or to teach the behaviors that will enable them to learn how to learn. Our question would then be: If not us, then who? If we are not satisfied with student behavior, and we believe that behavior is impacting student learning, then what are our options? Doing nothing? Doing the same things we have always done? Rather, we must collectively assume responsibility for improving behavior and collaboratively support students and one another. Improving student behavior is not easy, but it is possible. The social science behind improving behavior has a larger and more robust research base than any academic domain, with the possible exception of reading. It's not a lack of skill that will prevent success in this arena, but a lack of will.

Student motivation, or, more accurately, a lack of student motivation and engagement, is commonly mentioned as the reason for student difficulties, and as the reason for the failure of improvement efforts. However, educators can have an enormous impact on student motivation. Students are motivated and engaged when they believe that standards are relevant, when they have choice, when they have relationships with teachers, when they have opportunities to collaborate with peers, when teachers model effective social and academic behaviors, and when schools nurture a growth mindset. We can have a significant impact on student motivation if we accept responsibility for engaging students.

ASSESSMENT PARADOX

Educators have also become jaundiced about a critical but complicated topic in the teaching-learning process—assessment. RTI-based practices require evidence, but we face a paradox—many educators believe that we assess too much, and yet we do not possess the information required to inform our work. Educators also feel that they do not have time for assessments.

We recommend that all educators inventory the assessments that they are currently administering to check that the timely information that is needed to ensure that all students learn at high levels is being gathered, but without redundancies and inefficiencies.

Educators will benefit from embracing the notion that instruction and assessment are inextricably linked, and that checks for understanding and observations count and can inform instruction and grading. It is important to recognize that screening and pre-assessment, as is the case with other tests, can actually *save* time. Screening reveals which students have significant deficits that will almost certainly cause them to experience difficulties within the year, at some time and in some content area. Initiating supports immediately saves time and preserves students' belief in their own efficacy. Pre-assessing prior to units will reveal students who have gaps in their knowledge of immediate prerequisite skills—gaps that will likely necessitate interventions within the unit. We recommend that educators pre-teach prerequisites before and at the beginning of units to fill gaps, prepare students for success, and minimize the need to spend time later on interventions. Pre-assessments can also reveal that students already possess knowledge of content in upcoming units. By compacting content, educators can avoid wasting time on content students already understand, thereby allowing time for more depth of study or more practice with other content. Leaders must have conversations about these benefits with staff members who feel that there is not time for more assessment. And, they must help educators with the practical steps required to inventory assessments, link instruction and assessments, and screen and pre-assess in a successful way.

RTI-based practices will also inevitably raise the issue of fairness. Some teachers express the belief that it is not fair to other students— students who passed the test the first time—when we allow multiple opportunities for students to take a test. And some teachers feel that we are not teaching responsibility when we allow multiple opportunities. Educators have an important decision to make, because a firm commitment to all students learning at high levels and a firm commitment to only one chance to demonstrate that learning are entirely incompatible. We all recognize, as parents, caregivers, and/or teachers, that children rarely learn at the same rate and in the same manner. To terminate instruction at an arbitrary date and suggest that learning of that content is at an end, and the one-time opportunity to demonstrate mastery is upon us, defies all logic. But what about teaching responsibility? It is our position that responsibility is better taught by demanding that students persevere until they succeed than by giving them only one chance to do so. What are we teaching students when we communicate that they don't have to actually learn the content being assessed once they've failed that first test—that they are off the hook and need not keep trying? Does it not teach responsibility when we demand that students keep up with the new content *and* receive additional support on the old content until they reach the level of understanding needed for them to be successful? We are teaching children perseverance; we are insisting that they learn how to learn, and continuously strive to improve. The "real world" in which there are no second chances for which some teachers think they are preparing students is a myth. Colleges and universities increasingly embed multiple layers of support for students. Careers have always provided multiple opportunities to enter professions: multiple chances to pass the state teaching exam; multiple opportunities to pass the bar; multiple opportunities to revise the thesis or dissertation. It will not be easy, and it will take collaborative action to design a system that provides remediation and allows for additional chances to take assessments. However, we cannot continue to defend a stance that denies the reality of the ways and rates at which individuals learn. It is disingenuous, or worse, to craft mission statements that promise high levels of learning for all if we retain the fine print that expresses that there will be no second chances for the 5- to 18-year-olds we serve.

Conversations about fairness often address the specific question of how many chances students should receive to behave, to learn, or to be successful. The simple answer is, as many chances as it takes. In response to questions about fairness, questions that almost seem rhetorical, we are inclined to ask the questioner, "What are the other options? To give up? To dismiss the student from school? To break the news to parents that we cannot help their child learn?"

Our experiences have taught us that educators will almost never administer the same test repeatedly without ultimately experiencing success. They may, for example, recognize during the process that students' difficulties with demonstrating mastery of content reveal something about the method of instruction; adjusting instruction, even for one student, may make the difference. Or they may realize that some students *do* understand the concept and content, but cannot express their mastery in the form in which they are being assessed. For example, an oral examination may need to replace the written one. This is not to suggest that we will not hold those students and ourselves accountable for improved written expression, but if the learning target is related to identifying cause and effect in a story or analyzing the process of meiosis, the manner in which the students meet the learning target is of secondary importance. Lastly, a student's repeated inability to master a concept on a test may help educators diagnose a more fundamental need, perhaps an auditory processing deficit or a challenge with short-term memory. Once that need is discovered, the teacher can support the student in that area and subsequent instruction and assessment will result in more success.

GRADING DISPUTES

Another topic that will inevitably emerge, and that must be anticipated and addressed, is grading. There are two misunderstandings about assessment and grading within schools (Marzano, 2006). The first misunderstanding is that instruction is distinct from assessment. For example, "I taught the content for a week, and then I gave students a test." There is an unfortunate reluctance to assess students during the course of instruction, perhaps because teachers feel that they are unqualified to craft a valid assessment and they believe that the informal evidence gathered during the course of instruction is unreliable and invalid to inform teaching and impossible to use when assigning grades. This is simply not the case. We recommend that teachers and students move from assessment *of* learning to assessment *for* learning and even assessment *as* learning.

The second misunderstanding follows from the first: that assessing for instruction and assessing for the purpose of determining a grade are distinct. In fact, assessment is assessment, and the information gathered during both informal and formal assessments can be used for a variety of important purposes.

Grades should reflect what students learn, not how many points that they earn. Many schools, particularly secondary schools, continue to use letter grades that are calculated based on the number of points that students have accumulated in tasks such as completing homework, participating in class, or completing extra credit assignments such as attending the school play in addition to their performance on assessments of standards mastery, but this practice is incompatible with a mission statement that embraces the idea that all students will master prioritized standards. When points are earned simply for the completion of work or tasks, it is possible for students who do not adequately demonstrate mastery on assessments to pass a class. Alternatively, when points come from sources unrelated to mastery of standards, it is possible for students to fail even when they have mastered content by the end of the grading period.

Standards-based grading practices can exist; college entrance requirements and high school transcripts do not make their use impossible. In fact, they are the only honest way of communicating student performance to stakeholders, including students and parents, in a transparent manner. It is misleading to assign a "D" or "F" to a student who, despite earning only 20 out of 100 points on the first assignment of the semester, earns 80 out of 100 on the next three assignments. However, given a traditional form of grading in which points are accumulated, this student would earn a 65 percent—a "D" or lower in most schools. It seems equally misleading to give a student a passing grade because they try hard and complete all their homework, or because we do not want to upset or anger their parents. Instead, educators should be communicating concerns early to parents and intervening within the semester immediately and with intensity.

School leaders must start by discussing the purpose of grading, grades, and report cards in their schools. We believe that staff members will conclude that the purpose is to communicate a student's current level of performance. As educators, we do not need to rely on averaged or calculated grades to validate this communication; we are professionals. We should rely on evidence of student learning, and that evidence can come from the information gathered from formal and informal assessments that we administer and analyze throughout a unit and school year.

RESOURCE SHORTAGES

Yet another common refrain from internal stakeholders is that the school does not possess the resources to successfully implement RTI-based practices. What can schools do? We recommend that school leaders inventory the resources they have on site—the human, material, and temporal resources—in other words, leaders must analyze how the people, programs, and time that are available are being utilized. Every dollar must be considered an instructional dollar. School leaders should ask, "Are we using our money as close to students as possible?" This may necessitate hard decisions, but they are decisions that must be made. Schools are unlikely to receive more money in the near future, so leaders must utilize their dollars in a wiser, more efficient manner.

Leaders can start by taking a look at where the school's money goes. Moreover, they must examine what the school already has, perhaps on shelves or in closets, that is not being utilized, or due to insufficient training is not being used optimally. In our experience, schools do not often have to spend new money for programs; there are often research-based programs already available that can be reintroduced or revitalized. Leaders must inventory these programs.

All staff members must enthusiastically collaborate to ensure the success of *all* students. This includes general education staff, special education staff, English language specialists, reading specialists, etc., on behalf of general education students with high levels of readiness, general education students with lower levels of readiness, special education students, English learners, etc. Leaders must rethink the way their colleagues' skills are being utilized if they are going to meet the differentiated needs of all students.

We can—and must—dedicate the time, money, and expertise necessary to meeting student needs. The question is whether we have the courage and the will to make hard decisions about how we organize the schedules of staff members and students.

SECTION 3
SUMMARY

The difference between success and a slow, painful death for any new initiative is significantly impacted by the systems that are in place to monitor and sustain those efforts. We believe that the steps to success described in this chapter will ensure that the structures exist to support school teams in their journey. Structures are critical; culture is key.

Leaders must have the courage to address the most fundamental questions that some educators have regarding students: Can they really *all* learn at high levels? We now know neurobiologically, as we have long known behaviorally or experientially, that every student can learn. On the neurobiological front, studies of functional magnetic resonance imaging (fMRI), which measures brain activity, and electroencephalography (EEG), which maps electrical activity in the brain, have revealed that the "appropriate" parts of brains change as a result of high-quality instruction and intervention. Every educator has experienced a student who learns "despite" the most significant obstacles imaginable.

Our favorite story is Christopher, a severely autistic student who was also mute—his parents had never heard him speak coherently. When we last worked with Christopher, he was in a sixth-grade classroom for severely and profoundly disabled students and was reading solidly at a third-grade level. How? It starts with his teacher, Rachel, and involved sign language and a commonly utilized alternative reading program called Edmark. In our opinion, Christopher's success had more to do with school culture and with staff members' belief in themselves and in Christopher than with any structures or programs.

Yet, even if there remain doubts in some educators' minds regarding the probability that all students can learn at high levels, our only option is to put forth our best efforts to help every student learn. We cannot advocate learning for *some* students. Which students would we choose? Ethically, our profession demands that we expect the very best from ourselves and from all students at all times. Leaders and educators who do not launch every school year and school day with the firm belief that 100 percent of students will learn at high levels are doomed before they have begun.

WHAT DOES STUDENT EVIDENCE REVEAL?

The journey to RTI implementation has, up to this point, been based on historical evidence. Our own experience and the research of others in the field of education have informed the plans we have laid out in the RTI Roadmap. In this section, the types of evidence that school teams need to actively gather, analyze, and utilize to continuously improve are described. School decisions can and should increasingly be driven by the timely evidence that we produce. This section will detail those types of evidence.

Initiatives cannot be judged successful simply because we implement them; they must positively impact student learning and outcomes. Frequent, accurate, and appropriate information about the efficacy of initiatives is required to justify the effort needed to sustain them. A robust and effective RTI model demands information. Evidence, provided through formal and informal assessments, is the engine that drives education and RTI. We suggest that schools gather the types of evidence that:

- ► Identify students with significant gaps in foundational behavioral and academic prerequisite skills—this evidence is commonly gathered through screeners.

- ► Determine the extent to which students are responding to core content—this evidence is commonly gathered through common formative assessments (CFAs) and authentic performance tasks.

- ► Identify the causes or prerequisite skills that most frequently contribute to student difficulties—this evidence is commonly gathered through diagnostics.

► Determine the extent to which students are responding to Tier 2 and Tier 3 interventions—this evidence is commonly gathered through progress monitoring.

Identifying and administering assessments is not enough. Teams must ensure that they are gathering, analyzing, and utilizing evidence garnered from assessments to inform teaching practices and impact student learning. Figure 4.1 describes various types of student evidence.

FIGURE 4.1	Types of Student Evidence			
	Screeners	**Common Formative Assessments and Authentic Performance Tasks**	**Progress Monitoring**	**Diagnostics**
Why?	Identify students with deficits in foundational prerequisite skills	Determine the efficacy of core Tier 1 instruction	Determine the efficacy of interventions; determine the extent to which students are responding to intervention	Determine why a student is experiencing difficulties; examine the specific areas in which the student most needs support
Who?	All students	All students	Students receiving supplemental supports	Students not yet responding to instruction and intervention; students about whom we need additional information
How often?	At least annually; often three times per year	Short cycle; several times per unit	Every week or two weeks	As often as needed to inform supplemental supports
What does it assess?	Broad domains	Essential content	The skills or targets with which students are receiving more time and alternative supports (Tier 2); the domain in which the student is receiving support (Tier 3)	Specific, prerequisite skills which are likely contributing to difficulties

| FIGURE 4.1 | Types of Student Evidence *(continued)* |

	Screeners	Common Formative Assessments and Authentic Performance Tasks	Progress Monitoring	Diagnostics
On which students or groups does it focus?	All students	Students within a grade level, course, or class	Students receiving supports within small groups	Individual students
What does it inform?	Tier 3 supports; scaffolds required for students to access Tier 1 content	Tier 1 and 2 supports	Tier 2 and 3 supports	Tier 3 (and perhaps 2) supports
How is it used?	Identify which students require the most intensive supports; determine who will require significant scaffolds to access core content	Determine team's success in ensuring students master prioritized content; enable teams to learn from one another about effective practices; identify students who require more time and alternative supports to master essential content; identify the skills with which all students, and specific students, require more time and alterative supports	Validate the efficacy of interventions; ensure that students are responding to interventions	Determine which supports will most target student needs

SCREENERS

"Universal screening" is a popular RTI term. What does it mean? Screeners filter those students who are at desperate risk of failure unless they receive immediate, intensive supports. If it's predictable, it's preventable. We can predict who these students are—they scored in the lowest performance band on the state test; they scored in the 6th percentile on a norm-referenced test; they were suspended for 12 days last year. A strong RTI approach is predicated on the notion of prevention as opposed to the historical approach of waiting until a student fails and then launching a rescue mission. RTI does not rely on special education as the only intervention, but provides supports immediately upon the first hint of difficulty. All students are screened to identify any individuals who, despite a strong core instructional program (Tier 1), are still in danger of failure. To ensure that students do not fall further and further behind, students must have access to immediate help (Buffum, Mattos, and Weber, 2009, 2010, and 2012; Hierck, Coleman, and Weber, 2011). When RTI is implemented well, all students undergo academic and behavior screening. Those determined to be at risk for experiencing significant difficulties receive targeted, evidence-based interventions as soon as is practical.

According to Jenkins (2003), screening approaches should satisfy three criteria: First, they must clearly distinguish individuals who require intervention. Practicality is the second criterion for an ideal screening mechanism and requires that the process be brief and simple enough to be implemented reliably. Educators must perceive the effort to screen as reasonable and not onerous. Third, an ideal screening system must have a net positive effect; students identified as at risk for failure receive timely and effective interventions. Jenkins and Johnson suggest in an article on the RTI Action Network Web site three steps to selecting a quality screener: define the future outcome the screener seeks to predict, identify early predictors of later outcomes, and determine a cut-score on the screening measure that identifies students at risk.

As an example, let's consider a student being screened in the behavior domain. Schools and teachers may screen all students in the area of internalizing and externalizing behaviors using the Student Risk Screening Scale (SRSS) and the Student Internalizing Behavior Screening Scale (SIBSS). Completed at the conclusion of a school year by staff who know students well, data from these screeners could be leveraged to provide supports to students upon the very beginning of the next school year, before another year of difficulties is allowed to occur. They require little time to complete and students with behavioral needs above a given threshold will very likely require immediate, positive, and structured behavioral support at the start of the following year to be successful.

COMMON FORMATIVE ASSESSMENTS

A common formative assessment (CFA) can be defined as any assessment given by two or more instructors with the intention of collaboratively examining the results for shared learning, instructional planning for individual students, and modifications to curriculum, instruction, and/or assessment. They are teacher-created (or teacher-selected), teacher-owned assessments that are collaboratively scored and that provide immediate feedback to students and teachers. Ainsworth and Viegut (2006) suggest, "Common formative assessments [provide] regular and timely feedback regarding student attainment of the most critical standards . . . [and] also foster consistent expectations and priorities within a grade level, course, and department regarding standards, instruction, and assessment. . . . Most importantly, common formative assessment results enable educators to diagnose student learning needs accurately in time to make instructional modifications" (pp. 95–96). Reeves (2004) states, "Schools with the greatest improvements in student achievement consistently used common assessments" (p. 164). As we assess how students are progressing towards mastering the identified Priority Standards, evidence from CFAs reveals to teachers where they need to differentiate and adjust instruction to ensure this outcome is met.

CFAs are constructed to assess the key learning outcomes of "unwrapped" Priority Standards (Ainsworth, 2003a and 2003b). To be useful and valid, CFAs must meet several criteria:

1. A proficient score must accurately indicate that a student has learned.

2. A low score should indicate that a student needs additional support.

3. Analyses of errors must help Data Teams efficiently determine student needs and target intervention.

Collaborative analyses of CFA results by Data Teams can inform future practice. Specifically, Data Teams will know:

- ► To what extent—with what success—did the team guide all students toward mastery?

- ► What concepts or skills need to be reviewed with the entire class?

- ► What factors have contributed to student difficulties?

- ► What additional strategies/resources are needed to ensure students improve their mastery?

- ► What patterns can be identified from student errors?

- ► Among Data Team members, which instructional strategies proved to be most effective?

- ► Among Data Team members, which instructional strategies proved *not* to be effective?

- ► How can the assessment be improved?

- ► Which students need more time and an alternative approach?

- ► With which standards and skills do these students need more time and an alternative approach?

Data Teams' analyses can and must lead to planning the supplemental supports that some students, inevitably, will need. This planning will address the following questions:

► What interventions will be provided to these students?

► When will these interventions be provided?

► Who will provide these interventions?

► What strategies or resources will be used in these interventions?

► How will student progress be monitored to measure the effectiveness of these interventions?

Data Teams drive Tier 2 RTI, and their use of CFA evidence to inform instruction can lead to incredibly dramatic gains in student learning (Bloom, 1984; Black and Wiliam, 1998; Meisels, et al., 2003; Rodriguez, 2004; Hattie, 2009). Data Teams follow a specific step-by-step process to examine student work, apply effective strategies within both instruction and intervention blocks, and monitor student learning in response to strategies and interventions:

1. Collect and chart/display the data

2. Analyze the data and prioritize needs

3. Establish SMART goals (Specific, Measurable, Attainable, Relevant, and Time-bound)

4. Select instructional strategies

5. Determine results indicators

6. Review and revise

Monitoring and evaluating results and using those results to inform instruction is inherent in the Data Teams process. Data Teams require strong leadership to provide guidance, direction, vision, support, and feedback throughout the collaborative inquiry cycle. The collaborative practices of Data Teams align well with the major aspects of a strong RTI approach.

Tier 1 in RTI calls for high-quality, differentiated instruction for all students. Data Teams collaboratively examine evidence of student response to academic and behavioral supports to identify which instructional strategies have met student needs. When a student does not respond to focused, differentiated core instruction, schools must be prepared to supplement core instruction through Tier 2 supports, whether the needs are academic, behavioral, or both. The collaborative planning and analysis of common formative assessment evidence by all staff members guides Tier 2 supplemental time and use of alternative strategies that will support students.

The steps that guide the work of Data Teams ensure that teachers' instructional decisions lead to increasingly high levels of learning for all students. When individual students are found to have not demonstrated the levels of mastery that the Data Teams expect—in other words, when Tier 2 supports are required—we recommend that teachers augment the steps above with these Data Team Tier 2 RTI questions:

1. Which students have not yet mastered prioritized content?

2. With which specific skills does each student require more time and an alternative approach to gain greater mastery?

3. Why does the Data Team believe that this specific skill has not been mastered? (May include both academic and behavioral causes.)

4. What strategies does the Data Team feel will best address this skill deficit?

5. When will these Tier 2 interventions be provided? By whom?

6. What tool will the Data Team use to confirm that the student has now mastered prioritized content? By when?

As student needs suggest that Tier 2 or 3 supports are required, schools respond quickly, consistently, and efficiently with targeted supports. Whether this means more time, different approaches, more targeted supports, or interventions that address gaps in foundational skills, the response must be derived from the data collected and the collaborative planning of staff members who connect to the student. It's also important to remember that the high-quality, Tier 1 core instruction is still part of the Tier 2 or 3 student's program. The additional interventions serve to augment this quality work, not supplant it.

Data Teams are a fundamental component of RTI and are principle drivers on the journey to implement and sustain an RTI program. Augmenting the Data Teams process steps with the guiding questions above can enhance the teams' capacities to meet student needs. An example of a Data Team dialogue follows.

Data Team Dialogue

The fifth-grade math team gathers to talk about the results of the pre-test they just administered on the topic of adding and subtracting fractions with like and unlike denominators. The results show that 30 percent of the students achieved "proficient" scores, with the rest of the class scoring at the "far from proficient" level. One of the team members had taken responsibility for collecting and charting the data, and it is available for all to see at the start of the meeting. The team members then engage in dialogue about what they see as strengths and challenges for the students. They agree that students are able to add and subtract fractions with like denominators and appear to be fluent in finding the least common multiple. The data also lead them to believe that their teaching should focus on the need to identify a common denominator when adding or subtracting fractions and on converting fractions once the common denominator has been achieved. The team establishes a SMART goal for the unit and has determined that "the percentage of students scoring at the proficient level and higher on the fraction addition/subtraction post-assessment will increase from the 30 percent who did so on the pre-test to 80 percent, as measured by the teacher-made fraction addition and subtraction post-assessment. The discussion shifts to instructional strategies and the team agrees to provide extension work for students who have mastered the skill, and spend extra time providing direct instruction and extra practice for students who are not proficient. Some suggestions they have at this stage include:

- ► Have students play a fraction addition and subtraction game online.
- ► Review the introductory mini-lesson with small groups.
- ► Teach the mini-lesson and complete a practice sheet on finding common denominators.
- ► Set up peer-to-peer grouping where the proficient students work with those approaching proficiency, while the teacher works with the students most in need.

As the meeting time concludes, the team establishes what they will use as results indicators. They expect that the post-assessment results will be significantly higher than the pre-test results, as noted above. Beyond that, they also want to observe their students conceptually representing adding fractions using visual models, to observe students going through each of the steps to add and subtract fractions, and to ensure that they are engaged in each of the learning experiences that are built into the unit.

DIAGNOSTICS

Diagnostic assessments identify a student's needs in relation to the content or domain in which educators have determined that the student has difficulties. They are administered to at-risk students on an individual basis. These assessments provide specific and in-depth information that assists in targeting the interventions that will allow students to close the gaps in their learning. While their relative length likely precludes their administration to all students, they serve an essential purpose in assisting teachers in planning targeted and effective instruction and interventions. The use of diagnostics should be restricted to when they can provide either new, or more reliable, information about a child's academic or behavioral needs. It is important to weigh the potential value of the information that could be mined against the time required to administer a comprehensive diagnostic test. In our experience, schools, typically at the primary grades, sometimes use longer, diagnostic-like assessments with all students, calling these assessments "screeners." While these assessments are valuable and fulfill a role in schools, we feel these 20- to 30-minute assessments should be reserved for use as diagnostics.

A behavioral diagnostic could be a simplified Functional Behavioral Analysis (FBA) given to a student who has been identified with behavioral difficulties. The FBA would reveal antecedents that may be contributing factors to the misbehavior being displayed. If a student acts out when being asked to work collaboratively on a task involving reading, the teacher may adjust the requirement, have them select their partner, or temporarily provide an alternate assignment.

PROGRESS MONITORING

Progress-monitoring assessments measure the extent to which students are responding to supplemental interventions. They also ensure that the right interventions have been chosen for a student or a group of students. CFAs and progress-monitoring assessments share quite a few attributes. While CFAs determine all students' responses to core Tier 1 instruction, and in alternative forms, students' responses to Tier 2 interventions, progress-monitoring assessments determine the responses of at-risk students to the most intensive interventions. Teachers collect student performance data from progress monitoring on a regular basis, and plot results over time. Drawing a line of best fit through student scores provides an indication of the rate of improvement, or lack of improvement, that the student is making toward achieving mastery of specific skills.

Progress monitoring is an essential tool within a well-defined RTI practice. It assesses the adequacy of school supports as well as students' responses to these supports. Information can lead a team to conclude that a student needs a more intense level of support or decide that a student has responded to interventions and may be successful within a less intensive level of RTI support. Fuchs and Fuchs (2008) summarized the need for progress monitoring within RTI:

1. To determine whether primary prevention (i.e., the core instructional program) is working for a given student.

2. To distinguish adequate from inadequate response to intervention and thereby identify students likely to have a disability.

3. To inductively inform individualized instruction programs, by determining what does not work, to optimize learning for students likely to have learning disabilities.

4. To determine when the student's response to intervention indicates that a return to less intensive supports is possible.

Progress monitoring ensures that students receive the intensity of supports that they need to succeed. It also provides the evidence to justify removing supports when progress indicates that skill deficits have been ameliorated, so that students receive supports in the least restrictive levels of support.

A "check in/check-out" (CI/CO) process is used in the area of behavior to monitor progress—to determine if an intervention is working and the extent to which students are responding to intervention. In a CI/CO process, the teacher team, with administrative input and guidance, identifies a behavior that will be monitored daily or weekly with a simple rating scale that can be completed by both the student and teacher, with monitoring and mentoring provided by an adult with whom the student checks in and checks out. Revisions and decisions can be made regarding behavior based on CI/CO data just as revisions and decisions to academic supports can be made using more familiar progress-monitoring tools.

SECTION 4
SUMMARY

Data become evidence when educators use those data to plan next steps in the teaching and learning cycle. Analyzing the data generated by each type of assessment yields key information to assist educators in planning next steps and producing a targeted plan that promotes success for all students. Common formative assessments can validate the success of core instruction and inform future decisions; screeners help to identify which students will require the most intensive interventions to fill gaps in foundational skills; diagnostics help specify why students are experiencing difficulties; and progress monitoring informs educators and students about the impact of intervention. This comprehensive suite of assessments provides the evidence required to proceed along the RTI Roadmap.

WHAT'S THE MOST IMPORTANT TIER?

A standards-driven, well-defined, "unwrapped" Tier 1 informs all of RTI. Well-designed and intentional classroom instruction begins with a high-quality curriculum, but effective teachers do not simply teach such curriculum in a textbook-driven, page-by-page manner or in the same way for all students. Instead, they provide instruction designed to meet the specific needs of all students in the class, differentiating and enriching as informal and formal checks require.

Tier 1, or core instruction, should be driven by the strengths of the students in your class today—not last year's students, your best year's students, or the students you wish you had. Students' skills and attributes, combined with evidence-based instructional strategies and scaffolds, promote learning. Teachers create learning environments designed to maximize social and academic learning. Best practices reflect what will make a difference in student outcomes, not just the practices with which teachers feel most comfortable.

While there is no one-size-fits-all recipe that guarantees RTI success, effective schools in which we have worked share common features:

> ► All students who struggle academically or behaviorally receive high-quality instruction in general education settings. They are not pulled out of class and sent to special education or other self-contained settings. When they require supplemental supports, they receive them *in addition to* core instruction, not *instead of* core instruction.

► All instruction is evidence-based (we have evidence of student learning that validates that our practices are effective), practically applied, and can be validated as a best practice based on outcomes.

► All staff members (regular classroom teachers and other specialized teaching and support staff) work together in the planning and delivery of student instruction and in collecting and analyzing data about student performance.

► Data on student progress are collected, monitored, and analyzed across the curriculum (not just in isolated skill areas). Strengths are identified and built upon; areas of difficulty are addressed and improved.

► Student progress monitoring is ongoing, formative, and informative. There is neither reliance on one result to describe everything nor an overwhelming accumulation of data.

► The RTI approach is most effective when it simply becomes "the way we do things around here" and the work is seamlessly integrated into school-wide practices. Schools never stop "doing RTI"—the supporting practices of an effective RTI model drive all that educators do.

At Tier 1, these attributes provide the foundation for the work of everyone in a school. Typically when school teams struggle to provide effective Tier 2 and Tier 3 supports, it can be traced back to some of the key components of a solid Tier 1 approach being neglected. If the number of students requiring Tier 2 and Tier 3 supports seems high, it's likely that the problem resides in Tier 1 and not with having a "bad crop of kids this year."

Three key processes advocated by The Leadership and Learning Center support educators with the development of a comprehensive, universal Tier 1 approach. Rigorous Curriculum Design (RCD), common formative assessments (CFAs), and Data Teams are essential for schools as they create engaging, instructionally sound, and comprehensive units of instruction. These processes are described briefly in the following sections; they provide critical waypoints on the RTI Roadmap.

RIGOROUS CURRICULUM DESIGN

A deep understanding of mapping, instruction, and assessment within academic and behavioral domains will ensure more students learn at a deeper level during core instruction blocks. Figure 5.1 provides a summary of the key components of RCD.

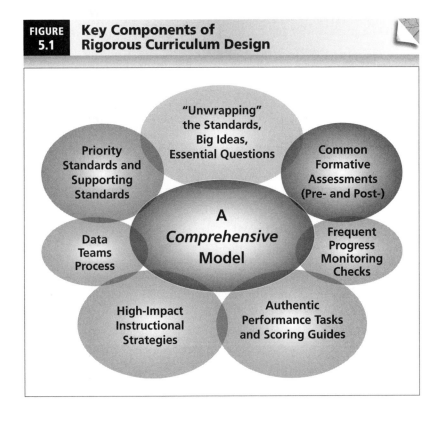

FIGURE 5.1 Key Components of Rigorous Curriculum Design

Rigorous Curriculum Design has two phases: building the foundation and designing the units of instruction.

Building the Foundation

Building the foundation consists of five steps (Ainsworth, 2010):

1. Prioritize the Standards

In this step, educators identify those Priority Standards that provide curricular focus and into which teachers will "dig deep." This is in contrast to supporting standards, which connect to and support Priority Standards. Educators use four criteria when prioritizing standards:

- ► Readiness for the next level of learning (within the course and between courses)
- ► Endurance of concepts or skills over time
- ► Leverage of concepts to other curricular areas
- ► Emphasis on external assessments (national, state, provincial, district, or division)

When contemplating a consistent approach to prioritizing standards that benefits all students, educators must consider the prerequisite skills with which students come to class. The identification of Priority Standards and the connection to subsequent learning is a key component of RTI.

2. Name the Units of Study

The unit of study can be defined as topical (with a focus on a specific portion of a larger subject or discipline), skill-based (with a focus on application), or thematic (with a focus on connections to other topics within the same discipline or other disciplines) and may last anywhere from two to six weeks. A key consideration for educators is to first determine the purpose and dominant focus of the unit, and then build the rest of the unit to best accomplish that purpose. As a result, a unit may occasionally be described by two of these terms. For example, a math unit may be topical (estimation) and also involve some application of skills (rounding).

3. Assign the Standards

Educators make the initial assignment of Priority Standards to the units according to each unit's focus as indicated in the naming step. Supporting standards are then assigned following the same approach. At this stage, it is critical to have a clear understanding of the intent of the unit. There may be occasions to have a Priority Standard span more than one unit in order for students to have multiple practice opportunities and achieve greater levels of depth of mastery. Similarly, supporting standards should enhance mastery of prioritized content and align with the theme of the unit.

4. Prepare a Pacing Calendar

A pacing calendar can be defined as the schedule for delivering all of the planned units of study for a designated grade level or course. Calendars do not define the daily instructional approach or materials that teachers will employ in delivering the lessons. Ainsworth (2010) states, "A carefully planned pacing calendar provides suggested horizontal learning progressions *within* grades and courses and suggested vertical learning progressions *between* grades and courses" (p. 79). Buffer time should be built within and between units to ensure opportunities to help students close any identified gaps. Marzano (2003) suggests the importance of the relationship between time and a guaranteed, viable curriculum: "In the current era of standards-driven curriculum, viability means ensuring that the articulated curriculum content for a given course or given grade level can be adequately addressed in the [instructional] time available" (p. 25). A well-designed pacing calendar assists in meeting the goal of viability for every student.

5. Construct a Unit Planning Organizer

A number of key components (including Priority Standards and supporting standards, assessments, scoring guides, and instructional strategies) should be included in the organizer. Organizers provide a place in which resources can reside, ensuring that effective, scaffolded, differentiated instruction occurs to meet the needs of all learners as part of a comprehensive Tier 1 approach.

Designing the Units of Study

Designing units of study involves a 12-step process. The steps are listed here and further details for each step are available in Ainsworth's comprehensive text, *Rigorous Curriculum Design* (2010):

1. "Unwrap" the Priority Standards—Analyze and deconstruct Priority Standards to uncover the teachable concepts and skills (the things students need to know and be able to do).

2. Create a graphic organizer—Once standards are "unwrapped," create a visual display (e.g., concept map, bulleted list, table, knowledge package) that lists the concepts and skills expected of students. Assign a level of rigor to each skill using Bloom's Taxonomy or Webb's Depth of Knowledge.

3. Determine the Big Ideas and Essential Questions— Determine the Big Ideas, or foundational understandings of the unit (what students should say they learned), and Essential Questions (which are designed to grab students' attention and prompt their thinking about the topic).

4. Create the end-of-unit post-assessment—Create the post-assessment, based on the "unwrapped" Priority Standards, which will serve as the guide for the unit; the post-assessment may be aligned with district or division benchmarks.

5. Create the pre-assessment—Create a pre-assessment to either mirror (same number and types of questions) or align (same types but fewer in number) to the post-assessment.

6. Identify vocabulary, interdisciplinary connections, and 21st-century learning skills—Identify specific vocabulary or technical terms that appear in the unit; make connections to other content areas and identify what learning skills are emphasized.

7. Plan engaging learning experiences—Generate authentic performance tasks with real-world connections that challenge students to think deeply and construct authentic responses.

8. Gather instructional resource materials—Select the appropriate print and technology resources that will help students process the "unwrapped" Priority Standards and generate the Big Ideas of the unit.

9. Recommend high-impact instructional strategies—Identify instructional strategies that will effectively deliver the content and allow for the differentiation and extension of the learning outcomes.

10. Produce a unit planning organizer—Specify the details (specific needs of specific students, learning progressions, strategies) needed to effectively teach this unit.

11. Create informal progress-monitoring checks—Design quick-check assessments for student understanding such as exit slips or tickets-out-the-door to gauge student understanding and adjust instruction if necessary.

12. Write weekly plans and design daily lessons—Create weekly plans to deliver the content of the "unwrapped" Priority Standards and daily lessons that align with weekly plans; determine when to best employ informal progress-monitoring checks.

Keeping in mind the nature of the students in a class will ensure that teachers process these steps with a discerning eye, ensuring that Tier 1 instruction is universal and designed for successful outcomes.

COMMON FORMATIVE ASSESSMENTS

Well-designed mapping-instruction-assessment cycles will more accurately inform tiered, supplemental supports and provide the data needed to inform targeted supports to students. Common formative assessments (CFAs) are the ideal, most research-based tools to measure student learning and validate the success of instruction and a viable, rigorously designed curriculum: they are efficient, promote equity, monitor and improve student learning, and inform and improve the practice of teachers. CFAs also help identify effective instructional strategies, which are essential to informing systematic Tier 2 interventions when students do not learn the first time. Collective reflections on CFAs ensure that increasingly accurate and reliable evidence is gathered to improve the collective efficacy of teacher team members. Assessments are discussed in greater detail in Section 4.

DATA TEAMS

"Data Teams" is a term coined by The Leadership and Learning Center to describe the process by which educators make data-driven decisions at the classroom level. They follow a specific step-by-step process to examine student work, apply effective instructional strategies and interventions, and monitor student learning in response to supplemental interventions. The Data Teams process was reviewed in the prior section. As a reminder, Data Teams:

1. Collect and chart the data: Teams gather and disaggregate data from common formative assessments.

2. Analyze data and prioritize needs: Teams identify the strengths and needs of students and prioritize the most urgent needs based on inferences drawn from the data.

3. Establish SMART (Specific, Measureable, Attainable, Relevant, Time-bound) goals: Teams engage in the SMART goal process and regularly review and revise these goals through their Data Team work.

4. Select instructional strategies: Analyses of the data guide educators in selecting the most appropriate strategies to use when intervening with students who have yet to master prioritized content.

5. Determine results indicators: Educators determine what measures will indicate that they have succeeded.

As the process starts over at Step 1 at the team's next meeting, the selected strategies are monitored for their impact. If student results are not improving, midcourse corrections are discussed and implemented.

6. Review and revise: Monitoring and evaluating progress to determine whether goals have been met is inherent in the Data Teams process.

In our experience, the school principal is the motivator and supporter of Data Teams and of making high levels of learning for all students a reality.

As Angela Peery (2011) notes, "When Data Teams are implemented effectively in a school, they are the vehicle that moves the school from a teaching organization to a learning organization" (p. 8). Collectively, we possess the expertise to meet all students' needs.

Whether used by Data Teams of teachers, or teams of administrators, specialists, and clinicians diagnosing the needs of students with more intensive needs, cycles of inquiry are the motor that ensures that more students are continuously learning at higher levels. Schools must ensure that teams meet regularly and communicate their find-ings efficiently to all relevant stakeholders.

SECTION 5
SUMMARY

We have worked with schools whose data indicate that a large number of students require Tier 2 or Tier 3 interventions. Schools have noted to us that they feel overwhelmed because more than 40 percent of their students require supplemental supports to master essential con-tent. Unfortunately, the conversation sometimes turns to the chal-lenges that students present as the rationale for the higher percentages. Collaborative conversations must instead examine the guaranteed and *viable* nature of the core curriculum, and the universal approaches being implemented to ensure success for all students. Tier 1 is the most important tier—defining, with clarity and specificity, the aca-demic and behavioral attributes that all students must possess is a fun-damental component of RTI. The Rigorous Curriculum Design, Common Formative Assessment, and Data Teams processes can en-sure that core supports are optimally successful in ensuring all stu-dents are on track to graduate ready for college or a skilled career.

WHAT ARE THE CRITICAL STRUCTURES OF AN RTI MODEL?

As schools develop and implement the structures of RTI, it is important to ensure that a culture exists in your school that supports high levels of learning for all students. The RTI Roadmap started by asking, "Where are we going?" Schools just like your school exist that are successfully serving students, schools in which the culture and the structures support continuous improvement and learning for adults and students. Mature and successful school models such as those featured in Section 1 show that it can be done; they inspire educators for the steps ahead, and reveal where gaps between current realities and the desired destination may lie. Schools that are successfully implementing RTI-based practices set their sights on college and career readiness for all students.

Section 2 addressed finding an answer to the question "Where are we?" This step requires courage and candor as schools examine the data and evidence that reflect current realities and states of readiness. What are the current strengths and needs of your staff and students? To what extent are all students responding to instruction? Are all staff members prepared to accept the change and temporary discomforts associated with RTI-based practices? Following reflection and study, school leaders must ask, "What are the next steps?" A school's RTI practice begins with the identification of realistic and optimally powerful first steps, based on the greatest areas of staff and student need and the highest-leverage solutions.

To ensure that educators' efforts are implemented so that student learning improves, Section 3 suggests that school teams must ask, "How are we going?" A 10-step plan that schools should follow to initiate, monitor, revise, and sustain RTI-based school improvement makes the journey more clear. These 10 steps define the benchmarks that must be met, and the way in which you can meet them, to ensure higher levels of student learning. They ensure that leaders monitor the progress of staff members, celebrate successes to motivate educators, and use interim evidence to make midcourse corrections. They prepare all stakeholders for the leadership and crucial conversations required of school staff members to hold one another accountable and ensure success.

Schools that maximize student outcomes through RTI-based practices thrive on evidence, which is discussed in detail in Section 4. Educators in such schools enthusiastically resolve the testing paradox—that we assess too much and yet we need more information about student needs. Evidence, provided through formal and informal assessments, is the engine that drives education and RTI. A balanced set of evidence-gathering tools includes those that:

- ▶ Identify students with significant gaps in foundational prerequisite skills, both behavioral and academic (screeners).
- ▶ Validate that students are learning the core content being taught during initial, scaffolded, differentiated instruction (common formative assessments).
- ▶ Reveal the antecedents to student difficulties—(diagnostics).
- ▶ Measure the extent to which students are responding to supplemental interventions (progress monitoring).

School leaders and educators must ensure that they are gathering, analyzing, and utilizing evidence to inform and impact student learning.

Less informed and less culturally sound schools interpret RTI as simply a rigid set of canned interventions, but Section 5 describes how schools engaged in deep, authentic RTI practices have definitively answered the question, "What's the most important tier?" Tier 1, designed and defined through a process of Rigorous Curriculum Design, Common Formative Assessments, and Data Teams, establishes the foundation for higher levels of student learning. A deep understanding of mapping, instruction, and assessment within academic and behavioral domains will ensure more students learn at deeper levels during core instruction blocks. Well-designed mapping-instruction-assessment cycles will more accurately inform tiered, supplemental supports.

These phases of the RTI Roadmap have prepared us for the final stage of our journey. To foster the construction of a system of supports, leaders must ask, "What are the critical structures of an RTI model?" Logistical questions related to school processes must be proactively addressed. This section will provide information and resources to address the following key questions:

1. Which students and student needs require more attention?

2. When will these supports be provided within the school day?

3. Which staff members are best positioned to provide supports?

4. Where will these supports be provided?

5. What resources, strategies, and/or programs are necessary to meet needs?

Collaborative, cooperative, and committed cultures are the foundations that sustain schools through the challenging and rewarding work of ensuring high levels of learning for all students (Buffum, Mattos, and Weber, 2009, 2010, and 2012; Hierck, Coleman, and Weber, 2011). The structures of RTI, as described in the following pages, are the bricks and mortar that build a foundation for RTI-based practices and the sparks that make RTI come alive for educators and students.

This section is about the *how* of Response to Intervention. While we believe that the *why* of RTI—the culture, beliefs, sense of urgency, and sense of "anything and everything it takes"—will always be more critical to a school's successful RTI-based practice, the logistics of RTI—the how—require attention. The best of intentions will be frustrated and success will be limited if educators do not systematically and efficiently address the following questions:

1. Which students and student needs require more attention?

Frequent data analysis, at both the Data Team and school-wide levels, is fundamental to RTI-based practices. Schools must have systems in place that:

> ► Screen to identify students with deficits in foundational skills.

> ► Frequently analyze common assessment data to identify students who have been experiencing difficulty in mastering essential grade-level or course standards.

> ► Frequently discuss at-risk students who have been screened or for whom common assessment data have revealed specific difficulties.

This question is critical—we cannot support students who are not on our radar screens. Educators must communicate with all their colleagues to ensure they know which students are at risk; to problem solve to diagnose why they are at risk; to ensure teachers are providing the most appropriate supports; and to validate that supports are resulting in adequate growth. In our experience, the obstacles to success related to this question include:

> ► Inadequate communication: To overcome this obstacle, use electronic forms that allow for asynchronous communication.

> ► Inadequate follow-through: To overcome this obstacle, meet face-to-face regularly, on a set schedule, to support staff members, to examine evidence of implementation and success, to ensure that stresses and workloads are manageable, and to provide the necessary information and resources so that success can be sustained.

2. When will these supports be provided within the school day?

Time is our most precious resource. Because we know that supplemental supports will best be provided within the regular school day, and because we should not remove students from core Tier 1 instruction to provide supports, the challenge of when to provide RTI-based interventions can paralyze implementation teams.

First, we recommend that schools strongly consider embedding a 30-minute daily (or 4 days per week, given that many schools have an alternative schedule one day per week to provide time for staff collaboration) intervention block. This time allows for differentiated Tier 2 supports for all students, in addition to those provided during Tier 1 blocks of instruction. Students who need more time and alternative supports to master essential content can receive that Tier 2 support during the 30-minute block without missing instruction in any other content. Students ready to go deeper and engage in problems and tasks of greater complexity can do so during the same block. When scheduled carefully, staff members can be freed to meet student needs during these time periods, potentially resulting in lower-than-normal class sizes. A fresh set of eyes is often helpful in examining schedules, to challenge the status quo and examine inefficiencies that may exist. Ability grouping often emerges during these discussions. We feel that a balanced approach is best, a viewpoint validated by the research (Hattie, 2009). During core Tier 1 blocks of instruction we recommend that students be grouped heterogeneously. During Tier 2 blocks of instruction, such as the 30-minute block described here, students can be grouped more homogenously based on need, with groupings revised as new evidence reveals the need for more time and alternative approaches for students to master a new set of essentials.

While well-designed and well-delivered Tier 1 and Tier 2 supports will meet the needs of many students—Bloom's (1968 and 1984) research placed the percentage at 95 percent—we will still have students who require intensive supports. Just as we can predict that some students will require a little more time and a different approach to master essentials, we can predict that a few students will require even more support to get on track to graduate ready for college or a skilled career. These students typically have significant deficits in foundational skills and will require systematic, intensive Tier 3 intervention. The dilemma is when to provide them. Consider these assertions:

► Students multiple grade levels behind their peers will not catch up in the absence of intensive, targeted supports.

► Students multiple grade levels behind their peers will likely fail classes and experience frustration and will not graduate from high school at all or will not graduate ready for college or a skilled career in the absence of intensive, targeted supports.

► Removing students from core literacy and mathematics instruction risks them falling behind in grade-level essentials as they learn skills from prior grade levels.

We believe that school leaders and educators must exercise the courage to commit to students who are desperately at risk. Literacy and numeracy are foundational, and their mastery is a civil right. Yes, students who struggle often find connections to school through elective courses, or highly contextual subject areas such as science and history. But is it not likely that these students would also feel greater connections to school if they experienced success? Is it not true that students' abilities to authentically and independently access the information presented in elective classes, science, and history are negatively impacted by illiteracy and innumeracy? Could it be that it's easier for us to justify lack of intensive supports, and easier to avoid the enormous challenges that arise when we attempt to ameliorate significant learning gaps, if we shelter ourselves and our students behind the notion that electives make them feel good about school?

The courage to accept responsibility for all students learning at high levels is based on:

► The deeply held belief that all students can learn.

► The recognition that literacy and numeracy are fundamental skills that can and should be prioritized.

► A commitment to the arts and sciences for all students, in conjunction with a commitment to build literacy and numeracy when illiteracy and innumeracy exists.

Students who are diagnosed with significant foundational deficits, and for whom intensive Tier 3 supports are deemed necessary and appropriate, can and must also have access to Tier 1 and 2 supports. Schools increasingly embracing this practice are designing schedules that include Tier 2 blocks of time for all students. When, though, can intensive Tier 3 supports be scheduled? These supports might need to be provided—temporarily, reluctantly, and flexibly—in place of other courses. In the model school examples in Section 1, these intensive supports were sometimes provided in place of science, social studies, or electives on a rotating basis. We recommend that schools discuss this issue openly and discuss the priority they place on content areas and skills within the school. It is important to relay that this is not a judgment on the value of individual staff members. Teachers of physical education, art, science, and social studies are teachers of children first, and children who lack literacy and numeracy skills are ill-prepared for later grade levels and for life. We cannot ignore this reality. The template in Figure 6.1 can be used to help educators determine the priority of various content areas.

We seek solutions that embrace the "genius of and," and avoid the "tyranny of or" at all costs (Collins, 2001). Students who require intensive, targeted Tier 3 supports—supports for which designated times are unlikely to exist—may need to miss another content area, but they need not always miss the same content area, and they need not miss all the content.

For example, schools, either elementary or secondary, may vary the time or the period during which intensive supports are provided,

FIGURE 6.1	Prioritize Content

Just as we prioritize standards within content areas, content areas must also be prioritized. Rank the most critical content areas and skills, with the highest-priority contents and skills at the top.

1	
2	
3	
4	
5	
6	
7	
8	
9	
10	

perhaps on a weekly basis. Thus, students requiring these supports, and the staff who provide them, may meet for Tier 3 sessions from 10:00–10:30 during Week A and from 1:00–1:30 during Week B. Because the remainder of the schedule remains fixed from week to week, students would not miss critical but less prioritized content for extended periods.

As another option, both elementary and secondary schools could provide Tier 3 supports during the "second halves" of instructional blocks. Students receiving Tier 3 interventions could then participate in the first phases of gradual release of responsibility lessons, leaving the class to receive Tier 3 supports while other students complete tasks independently or with peers. As with nearly all decisions about RTI-based practices, these examples require a cost-benefit analysis.

Tiered supports must be provided to students in need. Because extended days and extended years are not likely to materialize, we can and must creatively find time during the normal school day to provide these supports.

3. Which staff members are best positioned to provide supports?

Another precious resource within our schools is the staff members needed to provide intensive interventions. While we are excited about the potential of blended learning options and the uses of technology to instruct students, we will always need educators to support students, and this includes students requiring tiered supports.

As a rule, we want the most qualified staff members working with the students who are most at risk. Reality will dictate that availability will be another variable to consider, and this may mean that a less-than-optimally-qualified, but highly motivated staff member is providing supports. For this reason in particular, initial and ongoing professional development must be provided to any and all staff members serving as interventionists.

To find times during the day during which staff members may be available, or can be *made* available, to provide supports to small groups of students, we recommend that schools use a template such as the one in Figure 6.2.

The idea behind such a detailed analysis is not to suggest that staff members are not already working at maximum capacity; it simply recognizes that we will require all staff to consider working differently, more efficiently, and perhaps even in different capacities. We unfailingly respect educators' areas of strength and the contracts of bar-

FIGURE 6.2	Staff Availabilities													

List ALL Staff	8:00 – 8:30	8:30 – 9:00	9:00 – 9:30	9:30 – 10:00	10:00 – 10:30	10:30 – 11:00	11:00 – 11:30	11:30 – 12:00	12:00 – 12:30	12:30 – 1:00	1:00 – 1:30	1:30 – 2:00	2:00 – 2:30	2:30 – 3:00

gaining units; infringing upon rights is never a consideration. However, there may be 30 minutes of a staff member's day that can be repurposed to provide a targeted support. While we have worked with school secretaries with the will and skill to provide reading intervention to students, we recognize that this may not be a common circumstance. However, perhaps a staff member who is *not* primarily designated to provide instructional supports can complete a task within a 30-minute block of time that will free a staff member who *is* primarily designated to provide instructional supports to provide a daily intervention. Every 30-minute time block that can be freed up represents intensive, timely supports for children that would otherwise not be provided.

4. Where will these supports be provided?

While issues of *when* support will be provided and *who* will provide it perhaps represent more precious types of resources, space is also typically at a premium in most schools, so *where* supports will be provided also must be considered. When separate rooms cannot be designated as learning centers in which interventions can be provided, space must be identified more creatively. We work in schools in which hallways and small rooms serve as makeshift intervention rooms. Portions of classrooms can also serve as intervention spaces for a portion of the day; interventionists can commandeer a small table or rug in the corner of another staff member's room to provide support to a small group.

5. What resources, strategies, and/or programs are necessary to meet student needs?

We firmly believe that *what* educators use with at-risk students need not represent as great a challenge as questions associated with *when* and *who*. We simply believe in the power of adults to effect change; we believe that *how* we utilize materials will always be more important than the materials themselves.

This is not to suggest that we should ignore the importance of high-quality resources, strategies, or programs. Carving out time to provide supports and identifying a staff member to provide the supports will likely require a great deal of compromise and effort; do not neglect the *what*.

Potentially powerful materials can often be found lying dormant within schools and districts, and when they are not, they can be acquired at reasonable costs. The first step is to identify targeted supports that most specifically meet diagnosed student needs. Homework club, for example, is an appropriate support for a student who needs a safe, structured environment in which to complete work—a student who needs to be nudged to refocus from time to time. But homework club is not an effective support for students who require explicit reading interventions. Similarly, a reciprocal teaching-based guided reading group, in which a dedicated interventionist reinforces comprehension skills with students with significant reading deficits, will likely benefit students, particularly when texts are rich and at the students' instructional levels; however, if the primary area of deficit for these students is phonics, there may be more appropriate resources, strategies, programs, or supports to use.

We recommend that school leaders begin their identification of *what* resources are needed by drawing upon the skills and experiences of their staff members. Effective interventions often fall out of favor, or are only used in special education settings, or have only been thought to be appropriate in certain grade levels. In other words, appropriate interventions may already be present in your school. Collectively examine current and past practices to inventory what exists at your school. School districts rarely discard materials, and most have warehouses full of the favored programs of years gone by. Visit your district offices and chat with district "historians" to determine if "old" programs can be resuscitated. Finally, examine the evidence of staff success, both within and outside your school, and ask "superstars" to share the resources, strategies, and programs that they use.

In general, Tier 2 supports will not require additional material resources. Bloom's mastery learning (Bloom, 1968 and 1984) and DuFour's definitions of professional learning community practices (DuFour, DuFour, Eaker, and Many, 2010) both propose that Tier 2 represents more time and alternative strategies to support students in mastering grade-level and content essentials. Strategies need not cost money, are not best found in a program, and can be identified through an analysis of student performance. Are there staff members who have had relatively greater levels of success helping students master specific skills?

While Tier 2 supports typically involve supporting students in their efforts to master specific skills, Tier 3 supports are typically necessary because of deficits in broader domains of foundational skills that were likely an essential standard years ago. A fifth-grade student requiring Tier 2 supports may need a little more time due to difficulties identifying key events within a text from which causes and effects can be determined. A fifth-grade student requiring Tier 3 supports may have difficulty with cause and effect due to the inability to decode single-syllable words. Tier 3 supports typically require more time, more intensity, and more staff; students will benefit from a more scoped-and-sequenced, systematic set of materials. This often comes in the form of programs, some of which may already be present in your school or district. Use the form in Figure 6.3 to identify what your school already possesses and what you may need to acquire.

In the domain of behavior, purchasable programs are typically not the answer. Yet, there does exist a rich reservoir of research-based strategies from which educators can draw. Staff members are often strangely disappointed that a secret behavioral program does not exist. However, there are highly effective strategies that when used consistently and supported by other key elements of positive behavior will radically improve student behavior, and they are widely available. These strategies can be adopted from educators within your school and from sources within existing behavioral support systems. When completing the table in Figure 6.3, list the behavioral strategies that have proved most successful in your school and school district and that appear most frequently in the research and literature, and commit to using them more effectively and consistently.

FIGURE 6.3   Resources, Strategies, and/or Programs

Scour and glean items relevant to the domains in the chart from:
- All classrooms and closets within the school
- District office warehouses
- Other schools in the area

Log your findings in the chart.

Phonological Awareness							
Phonics							
Advanced Phonics							
Fluency							
Vocabulary/ Comprehension							
Early Numeracy							
Computation							
Behavior							

SECTION 6
SUMMARY

The cultures and structures associated with schools' RTI-based practices will continuously require leaders' and educators' attention. While school culture—the beliefs and attitudes of staff members—provides the foundation that prepares for and sustains the work, the structures are also critical components.

Ensuring that the structures of RTI practices are systematically and successfully in place requires that school leaders and educators address the following key questions:

▶ Which students and student needs require more attention?

▶ When will these supports be provided within the school day?

▶ Which staff members are best positioned to provide supports?

▶ Where will these supports be provided?

▶ What resources, strategies, and/or programs are necessary to meet student needs?

Although it requires knowledge and persistence, answering these questions is well within our capacity as professional educators. Asking the questions in a proactive and committed manner is the key to success.

Epilogue

The principles of Response to Intervention represent the most comprehensive, research-based, and logical procedures and practices in which schools can engage to ensure that all students graduate from high school ready for college or a skilled career. Our experiences with schools across the United States and Canada have led us to conclude that the educators in these schools embrace the notion that the principles of RTI are both necessary and representative of the ways in which schools should be functioning. School leaders accept the research-proven effectiveness of the elements of RTI and are increasingly seeking out specific guidance on how to begin or how to get better.

The RTI Roadmap is designed to provide that guidance. Through no fault of their own, school leaders may not know where to start, or what to do next, to improve their systematic supports for students. We hope that this book, *RTI Roadmap for School Leaders*, guides school teams through a collaborative process that nurtures a positive culture and builds the structures that support high levels of learning for every student. We recognize that all organizations, leaders, and professionals benefit from thought partners, particularly partners who understand the antecedents and evidence behind the practices they are looking to implement, and partners who have done, and are doing, the work. We will proudly and respectfully partner with any school interested in our support in utilizing the RTI Roadmap.

At the end of the journey described in this volume, we would like to reinforce a critical point—school culture matters. Governmental regulations, whether related to Response to Intervention or any other initiative, rarely mention the importance of culture. However, we are certain that six months into any new effort, the difficulties that schools face will relate more to the culture of the school than to the structures that have been established.

What do we mean by culture? A positive school culture is rich in trust and respect; there is recognition that collaborative processes are fundamental, that there is a collective commitment to effecting the changes that will produce positive outcomes. New initiatives are not repeatedly and haphazardly begun. Instead, depth (of student learning and of staff priorities) is valued over breadth. All students are valued and expected to make significant gains in their learning. Factors that may inhibit gains are viewed as temporary obstacles and challenges that will eventually be successfully overcome. All staff members accept responsibility for all students: students in other classrooms, students in other grade levels, students with disabilities, and students who speak another language at home. The status quo is never accepted; as expectations for students are appropriately raised, staff members recognize continuous improvement as the habit of great organizations. When areas for improvement are identified, change is accepted as an opportunity and all variables are considered. The prevalent attitude is "We'll do whatever it takes." School leaders and educators view adult behaviors as having the most effective and significant influence on student learning and behaviors.

We have observed practices in schools, districts, and divisions that have not led to positive cultures. Here are some common pitfalls:

▶ In our experience, top-down decisions will never result in sustainable change. While we believe strongly in the value of good leadership and in "leaders leading," we believe that all educators will agree that a balance of centralized (to organize, to guide, to facilitate communication) and decentralized (to provide input, to shape the actual products, to refine the work) decision making is the wisest, most respectful, and most productive way in which RTI, or any other powerful system, should be initiated. When decisions are made by fiat, from central offices or school offices, without meaningful input from stakeholders, RTI will often fail to reach its full potential. A collaborative approach to designing and implementing a system of supports for all students will more likely result in support from both principals and staff members; while this is critical, this approach involves much more. School-based staff members can identify what's working well, can accurately report current realities and states of readiness, and can report on areas where professional development is most needed.

▶ Leading change will take time. When change is rushed, perceived efficiencies associated with centralized strategies tend to dominate. Initiating change too quickly may also lead to insufficient time for stakeholders to study and process the proposed endeavor. Professional development may be rushed or attended to less thoroughly than is necessary. The most adequate resources may be missed and unnecessary compromises may be made. A surface application of the most basic aspects of RTI may be deemed sufficient as time takes precedence over meaning. We find that planning for RTI-based practices months or even a year in advance leads to the deepest, most successful, most sustained change.

▶ Staff members must receive initial and ongoing supports on RTI-based endeavors. We have observed many willing educators that struggle with tasks such as organizing their collaborative problem solving, diagnosing student needs, or monitoring progress because they did not receive an appropriate quality and/or quantity of professional development. Human, fiscal, and temporal resources must be budgeted to support educators in initiating and sustaining RTI.

▶ "Death by initiative" is a condition plaguing many school systems and organizations. A new idea or program every year, or seven new initiatives within a single year, is bound to leave staff feeling overwhelmed, and certain to guarantee that no idea is optimally employed on behalf of students. We understand the dilemma—there are many areas that need our attention, and there are many ideas and practices that would potentially benefit staff and students. We must, however, resist the temptation to introduce too much at one time. We must accept the likelihood that a single, wisely chosen initiative in one area of schooling can actually impact many of the areas in which students need support. The success of any endeavor—and the success of implementing RTI-based change in particular—requires that schools intensely focus on the most essential work. RTI cannot be one of many new initiatives and it cannot be this year's new initiative, to be followed by a new initiative every subsequent year. Initiative fatigue is a very real burden on staffs and schools. If we want to improve fully, deeply, and sustainably, we must focus. We feel that a focus on RTI is even more justifiable because we interpret Response to Intervention as synonymous with highly effective education. The characteristics of RTI, as described in this book and as practiced at schools across North America, involve all aspects of schooling—academics and behavior; curriculum, instruction, and assessment; and structures and cultures.

▶ Perhaps the greatest impediment to all students learning at the depth and complexity required to graduate ready for college or a skilled career is that we continue to attempt to cover an unrealistic number of standards. We must instead ensure that students master those standards that we have identified as the highest priority. We worry that there are students who have been diagnosed with a learning disability simply because educators have attempted to cover an unreasonable number of standards in a short period of time. A culture of coverage—as opposed to a culture of depth and mastery—plagues schools. Making matters worse is the fact that not all standards are created equal—they are simply not all equally important. While standards are important for defining the content that we will ensure students learn, we are in fact not teaching students standards—we are teaching students to solve problems and think critically. Some students may require more prerequisite supports to be provided; some students may require more time to master the most highly prioritized standards; all students will benefit from more opportunities to learn the most highly prioritized standards to greater levels of depth and complexity.

► Thus far we have only referred to academic skills. Educators are increasingly (thankfully) accepting responsibility for explicitly addressing students' behaviors, including social behaviors such as cooperation, respect, and responsibility, as well as academic behaviors such as time management, organization, and motivation. If we must provide students with explicit instruction in behaviors (and we must), then we must plan for greater focus of the academic content that we will ensure that all students master.

► The basic principles of RTI have occurred in isolated classrooms for as long as classrooms have existed. By our definition, however, interventions that are not provided systematically will not fully realize the potential of Response to Intervention. RTI must be built upon, and powered by, collaborative teams, and collaborative teams will most powerfully meet student needs by implementing the practices of RTI. Collaborative cultures—between teams of teachers, teachers and administrators, clinicians and teachers, general and special education, grade levels, and content areas are a prerequisite for successfully implementing RTI. Have a plan for how important information will be shared. Establish expectations and norms. Keep it simple, but remember to communicate.

▶ There is no Response to Intervention without monitoring. We must determine the extent to which students are responding. Insufficient monitoring will compromise the success of RTI, both for an individual student and for a school. School leaders must identify who will take the lead on monitoring, how frequently monitoring will occur, what tools will be used, and how results will be used. Results can motivate students and educators; they can inform adjustments to supports needed to make an individual student successful; and they can validate the success of interventions or suggest that interventions are not resulting in success for too many students. Data, information, and evidence make up the engine that drives RTI.

We have been fortunate enough to work at, and with, exceptional schools, school districts, and school divisions, and have observed practices that have greatly contributed to positive cultures. Best practices in the area of culture include:

▶ Schools and school leaders that have successfully led RTI-based initiatives have demonstrated a respect for change. Change creates anxiety because we fear failure, a loss of control, lack of support, personal impact, and the unknown. Knowing the potential resistance to change by some, and the reasons why change might be resisted, school leaders must: describe the *why* and *what* of change; present research on the change; provide time for stakeholders to reflect upon the change; provide staff members with the opportunity to voice opinions; describe the professional development for the new endeavor that will be provided and the ways in which the effectiveness of the new endeavor will be measured; determine whether consensus for the change exists; and then hold one another accountable for implementing the change. Change is a complex process that must be led with patient persistence.

► Like all initiatives, RTI must be implemented with transparency and trust. There is no such thing as too much communication. Leaders must continually and repeatedly describe why the change is necessary, what is expected (and what is not expected), and how successfully the change is progressing. We can anticipate that some stakeholders will have concerns and questions at some points during the implementation of RTI. We recommend that site, district, and division leaders schedule frequent times during which staff members can voice their concerns and questions, and during which leaders listen. Leadership and change require courage. Proposing change requires courage. Initiating the change requires courage. Holding colleagues accountable for change requires courage. Making modifications to the change requires courage. How can leaders muster the courage to lead? Often, courage is born of necessity. We believe that ensuring that all students graduate from high school ready for college or a skilled career is a social justice issue. It's an ethical and moral issue. It's a life and death issue.

Response to Intervention is organized passion—the passionate actions that embody the collective belief that all students will learn at high levels. Moreover, RTI represents the most comprehensive, research-based, and logical set of solutions that will ensure that students graduate from high school ready for life. There are not many educators with whom we interact who doubt the wisdom of implementing RTI. While a few of these committed colleagues report that they still come across educators who are intimidated by the changes required by 21st-century learning—and sometimes that intimidation can come across as reluctance toward change—most of our colleagues simply want a roadmap to guide them through the work. We hope that this book serves as such a guide.

References

Ainsworth, L. (2003a). *Power standards: Identifying the standards that matter the most.* Englewood, CO: Lead + Learn Press.

Ainsworth, L. (2003b). *"Unwrapping" the standards: A simple process to make standards manageable.* Englewood, CO: Lead + Learn Press.

Ainsworth, L. (2010). *Rigorous curriculum design: How to create curricular units of study that align standards, instruction, and assessment.* Englewood, CO: Lead + Learn Press.

Ainsworth, L., & Viegut, D. (2006). *Common formative assessments: How to connect standards-based instruction and assessment.* Thousand Oaks, CA: Corwin.

Bandura, A. (1977). *Social learning theory.* Englewood Cliffs, NJ: Prentice Hall.

Black, P., & Wiliam, D. (1998). Inside the black box: Raising standards through classroom assessment. *Phi Delta Kappan, 80*(2), 139–148.

Bloom, B. S. (1968). Learning for mastery. *Evaluation Comment, 1*(2). Los Angeles: UCLA Center for Study of Evaluation of Instructional Programs, 1–12.

Bloom. B. S. (1984, May). The search for methods of group instruction as effective as one-to-one tutoring. *Educational Leadership, 41*(8), 4–17.

Buffum, A., Mattos, M., & Weber, C. (2009). *Pyramid response to intervention: RtI, PLCs, and how to respond when students don't learn.* Bloomington, IN: Solution Tree.

Buffum, A., Mattos, M., & Weber, C. (2010). The why behind RTI. *Educational Leadership, 68*(2), 10–16.

Buffum, A., Mattos, M., & Weber, C. (2012). *Simplifying response to intervention: Four essential guiding principles.* Bloomington, IN: Solution Tree.

Collins, J. (2001). *Good to great: Why some companies make the leap . . . and other don't.* New York, NY: HarperCollins.

Collins, J. C., & Porras, J. I. (1994). *Built to last: Successful habits of visionary companies.* New York, NY: HarperCollins.

Conzemius, A. E., & Morganti-Fisher, T. (2012). *More than a SMART goal: Staying focused on student learning.* Bloomington, IN: Solution Tree.

DuFour, R., DuFour, R., Eaker, R., & Many, T. (2010). *Learning by doing: A handbook for professional learning communities at work* (2nd ed.). Bloomington, IN: Solution Tree.

Edmonds, R. (1979). Effective schools for the urban poor. *Educational Leadership, 37*(1), 15–24.

Fuchs, D., & Fuchs, L. S. (2006). Introduction to response to intervention: What, why, and how valid is it? *Reading Research Quarterly, 41*(1), 93–99.

Fuchs, L. S., & Fuchs, D. (2007). A model for implementing responsiveness to intervention. *Teaching Exceptional Children, 39*(5), 14–20.

Fuchs, L. S., & Fuchs, D. (2008). The role of assessment within the RTI framework. In D. Fuchs, L. S. Fuchs, & S. Vaughn (Eds.), *Response to intervention: A framework for reading educators* (pp. 27–49). Newark, DE: International Reading Association.

Fuchs, L. S., & Fuchs, D. (2009). On the importance of a unified model of responsiveness to intervention. *Child Development Perspectives, 3*(1), 41–43.

Fullan, M. (2010). *All systems go: The change imperative for whole system reform.* Thousand Oaks, CA: Corwin.

Hattie, J. (2009). *Visible learning: A synthesis of over 800 meta-analyses relating to student achievement.* New York, NY: Routledge.

Hierck, T., Coleman, C., & Weber, C. (2011). *Pyramid of behavior interventions: 7 keys to a positive learning environment.* Bloomington, IN: Solution Tree.

Jenkins, J. R. (2003, December). *Candidate measures for screening at-risk students.* Paper presented at the National Research Center on Learning Disabilities Responsiveness-to-Intervention symposium, Kansas City, MO. Retrieved from http://www.nrcld.org/symposium2003/jenkins/index.html

Jenkins, J. R., & Johnson, E. (n.d.). *Universal screening for reading problems: Why and how should we do this?* Retrieved from http://www.rtinetwork.org/essential/assessment/screening/reading problems

Kavale, K. A., Holdnack, J. A., & Mostert, M. P. (2005). Responsiveness to intervention and the identification of specific learning disability: A critique and alternative proposal. *Learning Disability Quarterly, 28*(2).

Lezotte, L. W. (1991). *Correlates of effective schools: The first and second generation.* Okemos, MI: Effective Schools Products.

Marzano, R. J. (2001). In T. Scherer, How and why standards can improve student achievement: A conversation with Robert J. Marzano. *Educational Leadership, 59*(1), 14–18.

Marzano, R. J. (2003). *What works in schools: Translating research into action.* Alexandria, VA: Association for Supervision and Curriculum Development.

Marzano, R. J. (2006). *Classroom assessment and grading that work.* Alexandria, VA: Association for Supervision and Curriculum Development.

Marzano, R. J., Pickering, D. J., & Pollock, J. E. (2001). *Classroom instruction that works: Research-based strategies for increasing student achievement.* Alexandria, VA: Association for Supervision and Curriculum Development.

Meisels, S. J., Atkins-Burnett, X., Xue, Y., Bickel, D., Son, S., & Nicholson, J. (2003). Creating a system of accountability: The impact of instructional assessment on elementary children's achievement test scores. *Education Policy Analysis Archives, 11*(9). Retrieved from http://epaa.asu.edu/epaa/v11n9/

Pausch, R., & Zaslow, J. (2008). *The last lecture.* New York, NY: Hyperion.

Peery, A. (2011). *The data teams experience: A guide for effective meetings.* Englewood, CO: Lead + Learn Press.

Peters, T. J., & Waterman Jr., R. H. (1982). *In search of excellence: Lessons from America's best-run companies.* New York, NY: HarperCollins.

Reeves, D. B. (2004). *Accountability for learning: How teachers and school leaders can take charge.* Alexandria, VA: Association for Supervision and Curriculum Development.

Rodriguez, M. C. (2004). The role of classroom assessment in student performance on TIMSS. *Applied Measurement in Education, 17*(1), 1–24.

Senge, P. M. (1990). *The fifth discipline: The art and practice of the learning organization.* New York, NY: Doubleday/Currency.

Statistic Brain. (2014). High school dropout statistics. Retrieved from http://www.statisticbrain.com/high-school-dropout-statistics/

Weiner, B. (2005). *Social motivation, justice, and the moral emotions: An attributional approach.* Mahwah, NJ: Lawrence Erlbaum Associates.

About the Authors

Tom Hierck has spent the last three years of his thirty-year educational career as a consultant and author travelling across Canada and the United States. His major focal points have been Response to Intervention (both academic and behavioral components), curriculum design, and school culture. This work has provided the basis for the eleven books he has authored or coauthored, including this latest book, *RTI Roadmap for School Leaders: Plan and Go*, with frequent collaborator Chris Weber. His work has also been translated into other languages as more educators look to improve and enhance their students' educational experience.

Tom's career, including time as a teacher, administrator, district leader, university sessional lecturer, department of education project leader, and executive director, has contributed to his unique perspective on education and the importance of positive learning environments to improve student learning. His belief that "every student is a success story waiting to be told" has led him to work with teachers and administrators to create positive school cultures and build effective relationships that facilitate learning for all students.

Tom and his wife, Ingrid, are the proud parents of three children and four grandchildren. Tom's passion for education and his desire to enhance learning environments has been fueled further since he became a grandparent. He wants to ensure that his grandchildren have the same high quality of education that he experienced.

Dr. Chris Weber has been in service to community and country his entire life. A graduate of the U.S. Air Force Academy, Chris flew C-141s during his military career. As a former high school, middle school, and elementary school teacher and administrator, Chris has had a great deal of success helping students who historically under-achieve learn at extraordinarily high levels.

As a principal and district office leader across California and in Chicago, Chris and his colleagues have developed systems of Response to Intervention that have led to heretofore unrealized levels of learning at schools across the country.

Chris is recognized as an expert in behavior, mathematics, and Response to Intervention. He consults and presents nationally to audiences on important educational topics.

Chris is the author of *Pyramid Response to Intervention: RtI, PLCs, and How to Respond When Students Don't Learn, Pyramid of Behavior Interventions: 7 Keys to a Positive Learning Environment, Simplifying Response to Intervention: Four Essential Guiding Principles, RTI in the Early Grades: Intervention Strategies for Mathematics, Literacy, Behavior & Fine-Motor Challenges.*

In addition to writing and consulting on educational topics, Chris continues to serve in schools, working with teachers and students every day in Chicago, Illinois, at some of the highest-performing urban schools in the nation.

Index